A Review of Research on Problematic Internet Use and Well-Being

With Recommendations for the U.S. Air Force

Joshua Breslau, Eyal Aharoni, Eric R. Pedersen, Laura L. Miller

RAND Project AIR FORCE

Prepared for the United States Air Force
Approved for public release; distribution unlimited

For more information on this publication, visit www.rand.org/t/RR849

Library of Congress Control Number: 2015935310

ISBN: 978-0-8330-8824-6

Published by the RAND Corporation, Santa Monica, Calif.

© Copyright 2015 RAND Corporation

RAND® is a registered trademark.

Support RAND
Make a tax-deductible charitable contribution at
www.rand.org/giving/contribute

www.rand.org

Preface

To help the Air Force understand the implications of the Internet, social media, and other information and communication technologies (ICTs) for Airmen's social support networks, mental health, suicide prevention programs, and outreach, RAND conducted a survey of 3,479 active-duty, guard, and reserve Airmen in 2012. Using survey responses weighted to represent the gender, age group, component and officer/enlisted composition of the force, RAND found that 6 percent of the sample scored on the negative end of the Generalized Problematic Internet Use Scale 2 (GPIUS2) (Caplan, 2010, pp. 1089–1097). This 15-item scale measures indicators of undesirable behavior such as turning to the Internet when feeling down or lonely, thinking obsessively about going online, having difficulty controlling Internet use, and experiencing adverse life events due to Internet use. Among Airmen, negative GPIUS2 scores were significantly correlated with poor self-rated mental health, depressed mood, and loneliness. If the survey results are representative, more than 30,000 Airmen may be struggling with unhealthy patterns of Internet use. These findings are documented in a previous RAND report, entitled, *Information and Communication Technologies To Promote Social And Psychological Well-Being In The Air Force: A 2012 Survey Of Airmen* (Miller, Martin, Yeung, Trujillo, and Timmer, 2014).

This report documents follow-on research providing the Air Force with a more in-depth review of the current state of knowledge on problematic Internet use (PIU), with special attention to populations and considerations most relevant for the military population and setting. It also draws implications for military leaders interested in potentially identifying, tracking, treating, or learning more about PIU within their organization. This report is written for both military and general readers. Subject-matter expertise is not required.

The research reported here was commissioned by the Air Force Office of the Surgeon General (AF/SG) and conducted within the Manpower, Personnel, and Training and Program of RAND Project AIR FORCE. The views here expressed do not necessarily reflect the official policy or position of the Department of the Air Force.

RAND Project AIR FORCE

RAND Project AIR FORCE (PAF), a division of the RAND Corporation, is the U.S. Air Force's federally funded research and development center for studies and analyses. PAF provides the Air Force with independent analyses of policy alternatives affecting the development, employment, combat readiness, and support of current and future air, space, and cyber forces. Research is conducted in four programs: Force Modernization and Employment;

Manpower, Personnel, and Training; Resource Management; and Strategy and Doctrine. The research reported here was prepared under contract FA7014-06-C-0001.

Additional information about PAF is available on our website:
http://www.rand.org/paf

Contents

Figure

Tables

Summary

Just as the Internet was becoming part of everyday life in the mid-1990s, mental health professionals started seeing patients who were so absorbed in their online activities that they were neglecting their important social relationships, their work responsibilities, and even their health. To some clinicians and researchers, it seemed that online activities could lead to dysfunctional behavior. Others even suggested that people could become "addicted" to the Internet, just as they become addicted to gambling or alcohol. As Internet use exploded in the ensuing decades, concern with what has been called problematic Internet use (PIU) or Internet addiction has also grown.

PIU is of concern to the Air Force because it presents new policy challenges. On the one hand, PIU may be particularly likely to emerge among the young adult male demographic of most Airmen. In fact, a 2012 RAND survey estimated that 6 percent of Airmen have PIU using a validated assessment tool. On the other hand, since PIU is a newly emerging condition, little is known about why it occurs, the severity of the impairment it causes, and strategies for preventing and treating it. Indeed, knowledge of PIU is uncommon even among mental health professionals. This report seeks to inform the development of Air Force policies aimed at mitigating PIU's impact on operations and the mental health of Airmen.

How Is PIU Defined, and How Prevalent Is It?

Although a variety of terms and measures have been used to assess PIU, it is commonly defined by symptoms associated with addiction, including excessive and compulsive use, tolerance, withdrawal, and impairment. Individuals with PIU use the Internet compulsively, continuing a pattern of excessive use despite adverse consequences or self-imposed limits. They develop tolerance, so their use becomes increasingly intensive or prolonged, and they have anxiety and other withdrawal symptoms when they cannot be online. Their everyday functioning is impaired, resulting in reduced productivity, friction with friends and family, and failure to perform basic activities. The specific problem activities vary widely. For example, for some, online gaming is the primary difficulty; for others it may be social media, chat rooms, pornography, or gambling.

Although PIU is broadly recognized as a highly problematic behavior pattern that warrants clinical attention, there is no consensus that it constitutes a distinct clinical diagnosis. Like other behavioral addictions, PIU is considered a disorder by some researchers and clinicians, but it is not recognized as such in the American Psychiatric Association's official catalog of disorders, the Diagnostic and Statistical Manual of Mental Disorders, Version 5 (DSM-5). This does not mean that most psychiatrists think that PIU is not a potentially serious condition warranting clinical attention. Many view PIU as a set of behaviors that may reflect an underlying psychiatric disorder such as depression. More research is needed in this area to determine whether PIU should be considered a distinct disorder with a unique etiology and treatment approach. Internet Gaming Disorder was included in an appendix to DSM5 for conditions that warrant additional research and clinical experience prior to consideration for inclusion as an official disorder.

The prevalence of PIU is difficult to gauge. The research to date has used small and often very specialized samples, different assessment tools, and inconsistent definitions and criteria. Also, because Internet penetration has expanded so rapidly, studies quickly become out of date. The most reliable study we found put the prevalence of PIU at less than 1 percent of the U.S. population in 2004, and this decade-old study was conducted well before the steep rise in the adoption of broadband Internet access, computer tablets and smartphones, and the rapid expansion of social media and smartphone "apps." As noted earlier, the 2012 RAND survey of U.S. Air Force military personnel estimated that 6 percent of Airmen may be struggling with PIU.

What Are the Risk Factors and Consequences?

It is unclear whether excessive Internet use results in the social and psychological issues associated with it or whether those issues make an individual vulnerable to PIU. However, it is clear that PIU does not often occur in isolation, and a variety of likely risk factors have been identified, including social withdrawal, victimization, emotional instability, aggression, anxiety, depression, substance abuse, and suicidal behavior.

The consequences of PIU can be life altering: for example, marital conflict or child neglect due to a spouse or parent spending free time engaging in cybersex or hanging out in chat rooms; financial difficulties because a compulsive shopper can now make purchases online 24 hours a day; ruined college careers because a student chooses gaming over studying and attending class; unemployment due to a worker's inability to stay off social media during work hours; and physical ills caused by sitting at a computer too long and not sleeping, eating, exercising, or even bathing sufficiently.

What Strategies Are Used for Prevention and Treatment?

Comprehensive prevention and treatment strategies include individuals at risk for PIU, their employers, and their clinicians. The following approaches have support in the existing literature:

Individuals at risk: Self-regulation strategies are likely to be the front line of PIU prevention. These include self-monitoring, committing to limited usage, and rewards for meeting goals. Many online tools are available for purchase and free of charge to block access to certain sites, limit usage of a site, or provide usage statistics. Because many job duties require Internet access, people need strategies to regulate their use of the specific websites associated with their problem.

Employers: Most employers already have Internet policies in place aimed at keeping workers productive. The standard response to violations has been discipline or termination, not taking into account the potential role of PIU in the employee's behavior. But some companies are developing "cyber wellness" programs designed to increase employee, supervisor, and management awareness of PIU issues, reduce incidents, and decrease the employer's liability in the case of a terminated employee claiming that the rules for Internet use were not clear or that he or she had a mental health problem.

Mental health clinicians: Over the past 25 years, clinicians have developed treatments for PIU based on existing and proven treatments for depression, anxiety disorders, and substance use disorders. However, the effectiveness of these treatments for PIU specifically has yet to be tested in rigorous clinical studies. The treatments show promise, but their use should be closely monitored and adjusted as the research grows richer. Among the more promising treatment candidates is cognitive-behavioral therapy, which is successful at treating anxiety disorders or depression. Principles of substance abuse treatment are also incorporated into treatments, including abstinence and "harm reduction"—reducing or limiting use, often after temporary abstinence. Harm reduction typically is more attractive and feasible than abstinence because Internet access is so essential to work and daily communication. In the absence of proven PIU-specific treatments, for now clinicians should consider PIU symptoms as potential manifestations of underlying disorders which can be treated using established methods.

Our Recommendations

Until the research on PIU matures, policies that promote education and awareness, self-monitoring, and efficient and private access to wellness services represent judicious steps toward successfully managing, and preventing this potentially debilitating condition. The overall goal of our recommendations is to shift the culture regarding Internet use in the Air Force so that the mental health aspects of Internet use, i.e., PIU and its common mental health comorbidities, are given appropriate priority in the operational awareness of leaders, workplace policies, and mental health treatment.

Increase awareness: Organizational leadership and mental health professionals should be trained to consider PIU as a factor influencing Airmen's behavior. Training should cover the signs of PIU and its association with mental health problems, as well as protocols for unobtrusive mental health referral. Content related to PIU should be included in existing commander handbooks and broader training programs related to Airmen's mental health and well-being.

Provide support on the job: As in the civilian sector, the Air Force could benefit by incorporating knowledge of PIU into Internet use policies. The Air Force as well as civilian employers should focus on voluntary monitoring; educational, prevention, and treatment services; and self-monitoring support. They should carefully weigh the pros and cons of more onerous policies that would broadly restrict Internet access and adversely affect overall productivity. They should also exercise caution when disciplining violators, taking into account that some may be in need of professional mental health services. Leaders should also recognize that while some Airmen may require Internet access to perform their duties, there are potential hazards to allowing access to the "drug of choice" for the Internet "addict," and that restrictions on access to selected problematic sites may be warranted. Relatively minor adjustments to workplace environment or work responsibilities may be sufficient to help some individuals with PIU remain on-task and productive.

Employ promising treatment approaches: Mental health treatment should be considered in cases where PIU persists despite attempts to help an individual self-regulate Internet use. Until more is known about tailoring treatment approaches to PIU, mental health professionals can follow civilian providers' lead in providing cognitive-behavioral therapy and elements of substance abuse treatment to Airmen suffering the consequences of PIU and associated disorders. Mental health practitioners should consider clinical assessments of PIU in their patients to help detect problems that might not otherwise surface. They are also likely to benefit from continuing education programs focused on PIU, as well as ensuring that they have a basic understanding of common technologies and associated terms (e.g., avatar, sexting, Internet troll) so they can better understand the experiences of the Airmen they are treating.

Continue to investigate PIU in the Air Force: Further investigation is sorely needed to understand PIU in the general population and in the military in particular. In the Air Force, a cost-effective method could include performing a quantitative assessment to measure PIU, perhaps as part of biennial Air Force Community Assessment surveys. This instrument offers the opportunity to assess prevalence as well as the relationship between PIU scores and other indicators of well-being. We recommend using language more broad than "Internet," as addiction-like behaviors regarding computer, smartphone and video game use more generally hold as much relevance for the military as the more narrowly focused term "Internet." Otherwise, measures can underestimate the problem if respondents do not think of time in an online game or on their smartphones as being "on the Internet."

Qualitative exploration to determine what PIU looks like in the military population could also provide context-specific information that would help develop better strategies to address it. For example, does PIU often follow a life event or begin during a certain military experience? Does it tend to start before Airmen join the service? What obstacles exist to overcoming PIU? How much do military leaders, chaplains, and mental health professionals know about it, and how do they attempt to address it? The results of a qualitative study could identify

- targeted topics to include in the large-scale survey to assess prevalence and track PIU over time
- misconceptions and counterproductive behaviors among personnel attempting to address PIU
- interest in or need for continuing education on the topic for military counselors
- military-specific examples of PIU for use in educational and training materials

- points of vulnerability where special outreach may be warranted (e.g., postdivorce, postcombat, during assignments to remote locations).

Acknowledgments

We thank the Air Force action officers and advisors in the Air Force Surgeon General's office who provided earlier feedback on the literature review and qualitative research design: Colonel Tracy Neal-Walden, Colonel Cherri Shireman, Major Elisha Parkhill, and Velda Johnson. Lieutenant Colonel Mike Foutch, an Air Force fellow at RAND during the fiscal year of this study, also provided valuable feedback and guidance along way, including perspectives that helped shape the recommended approach for qualitative research on the topic. This manuscript benefited from the editorial assistance of Melissa Bauman. Ray Conley and Kirsten Keller offered suggestions for improvement on an earlier draft of this manuscript. We are also grateful for the contributions of our peer reviewers, Scott Caplan and Charles Engel.

Abbreviations

ADHD	attention deficit hyperactivity disorder
AF	Air Force
CBT	cognitive-behavioral therapy
DSM5	Diagnostic and Statistical Manual of Mental Disorders 5
GPIU	generalized pathological Internet use
IAT	Internet Addiction Test
ICT	information and communication technology
PIU	problematic Internet use
RCT	randomized controlled trial
SPIU	specific pathological Internet use

Chapter One. Introduction

The Internet provides healthy people the opportunity for a variety of benefits, including social engagement, emotional support, skill development, financial gains, education, and entertainment. However, Internet activities have also been found to be related to problems with some users' daily functioning and psychosocial well-being, prompting clinicians and social scientists to attempt to understand and address this historically novel phenomenon. These problems came to the attention of mental health clinicians who began to see patients with difficulties controlling their Internet activities. The cases included college students who failed out of school due to constant Internet gaming that distracted them from their academic work, couples whose marital conflict stemmed from one partner spending excessive amounts of time in online chat rooms or engaging in online sexual activities, and adults whose compulsive online shopping or gambling has resulted in catastrophic financial problems.

As is not uncommon for a new field of inquiry, several terms for this phenomenon have emerged and are sometimes used interchangeably, including compulsive Internet use, pathological Internet use, excessive Internet use, Internet dependency, Internet addiction, cyberaddiction, and problematic Internet use. In this report, we review highlights from the body of research into this behavioral phenomenon, its definitions, associated factors, and candidate treatment strategies, with an emphasis on recent findings from U.S. samples. For this literature review, we favor the term "problematic Internet use" (PIU) because it makes fewer assumptions about the underlying pathology.

PIU is of considerable interest to the Air Force because it is an emerging mental health problem which may be particularly common among the young adult demographic of most Airmen and relatively unknown among more senior staff and mental health professionals. Prior RAND research found that 6 percent of Airmen self-reported behaviors indicative of PIU (Miller, Martin, Yeung, Trujillo, and Timmer, 2014). Moreover, PIU presents additional complexity for an institution such as the Air Force, where access to the Internet is nearly universal in many operational settings. While Internet use policies have developed with a primary focus on work productivity, the overlap between disciplinary problems and mental health problems remains challenging. The objective of this literature review is to draw lessons from the existing scientific literature that can guide Air Force policy through this emerging domain.

Methodology

Relevant scholarly literature was identified via a series of queries using popular citation indexes including EBSCOHost, Thomson Reuters' Web of Science, Google Scholar, and RAND library databases. Search terms included compulsive Internet use, pathological Internet use, excessive Internet use, Internet dependency, Internet addiction, cyberaddiction, and problematic Internet use. Priority was given to peer-reviewed empirical research and clinical articles within the past ten years and with particular relevance to adult, Western, organizational, and military populations. Relevant research was also identified through standard literature review practices, such as consulting with experts in the field for recommendations and pursuing publications cited in the articles obtained through online queries.

Organization of This Report

Chapter Two discusses terms, definitions, and measurements of PIU. Chapter Three reviews what is known about organizational prevention and management strategies, as well as treatment strategies for those with PIU. Chapter Four highlights caveats and limitations of the current literature and makes recommendations for the Air Force, taking those limitations into account.

Chapter Two. Understanding the Emerging Science of PIU

As ownership of personal computers began to grow during the 1980s, researchers began to explore anecdotal accounts and media stories describing individuals as "addicted" to their computers in the way that others are addicted to drugs (Shotten, 1989, 1991). Reports of similar behaviors related to online computer activities emerged just as the Internet began its dramatic expansion in the mid-1990s. Problematic Internet Use (PIU), the most general term applied to these cases, was first described in the scientific literature in the 1990s (Griffiths, 1996; Young, 1998). Since that time, concern with PIU has grown as the Internet has come to be a ubiquitous feature of modern life.

Since 2000, technological advances have made it easier for Americans to access the Internet anytime, anywhere, for extended periods of time. In 2000, 40 percent of American adults used a modem to "dial up" into a session on the Internet, while 3 percent subscribed to a high-speed, always-on broadband connection (Pew, 2014a). As of late 2013, 70 percent of Americans had adopted broadband connections, and only 2 percent still used dial-up (Pew, 2014a). The Internet has also become widely available outside the home due to the expansion of wireless connections and the adoption of laptops, smartphones, and tablet computers. As of January 2014, 87 percent of American adults use the Internet, and 46 percent say the Internet would be very hard or impossible to give up (Pew, 2014b).

As access to the Internet and its array of online activities has expanded, the research on PIU has also grown, with notable contributions from researchers in China and Korea, where PIU has become a high-profile issue framed as a public health problem, particularly among adolescents (Liu, 2012). In this chapter, we review this literature focusing on two sets of scientific questions. First, how have researchers defined PIU and measured its prevalence in the United States? What is the current scientific consensus on whether PIU is a distinct psychiatric disorder? Second, what are the risk factors for and consequences of PIU? What is the current model of how the behavior arises and has its adverse effects?

How Is PIU Defined?

Despite the large body of research, there is not yet a consensus in the field regarding a set of criteria for defining PIU (Chou, Condron, and Belland, 2005; Byun et al., 2009; Moreno et al., 2011; Ko et al., 2012). However, the criteria that have been used in research generally follow similar principles. Most commonly, PIU is defined using established concepts from addiction medicine. Substance addictions are generally defined by three classes of criteria: (1) compulsive use, meaning excessive use that continues despite adverse consequences and/or attempts to quit, (2) tolerance, meaning a need to consume greater quantities of a substance to achieve the same desired effect, and (3) withdrawal, meaning physiological symptoms or cravings for the substance after voluntary or involuntary abstinence. Research on PIU, much of which uses the term "Internet addiction," tends to focus on Internet use behaviors that correspond to these addiction criteria (Kuss, Griffiths, Karila, and Billieux, 2013). For instance, compulsive use of the Internet can be defined as staying online for very long periods of time while neglecting social responsibilities. Similarly, tolerance can be defined as increasing intensity of engagement with online activities, and withdrawal can be defined by symptoms of distress or acute changes in functioning that occur when a person is unable to go online.

While addiction has provided the dominant model for studies of PIU, researchers have also suggested connections between the symptoms of PIU and other types of psychiatric disorder (Ko, 2012). PIU may involve distractibility and difficulty focusing on work activities, symptoms that are characteristic of attention deficit hyperactivity disorder (ADHD). Not surprisingly, studies have found associations between ADHD and PIU (Ko et al., 2012). Other scholars have suggested that most cases of PIU might operate more like an impulse control disorder wherein people take risky actions, not because they are repeatedly compelled to seek a risky reward, but simply because they lack foresight about such risks (Davis, 2001; Shapira, 2003).

Finally, researchers have proposed an important distinction between two different types of PIU, one focused on specific activities that are conducted through the Internet, such as online gaming or viewing pornography, and one involving a generalized pattern of Internet use that is not restricted to a particular type of rewarding activity. In cases of the former, sometimes called specific pathological Internet use (SPIU), individuals are engaged in activities that are commonly conducted offline as well as online, with the Internet simply providing a means of access to the goal (Davis, 2001; King, Delfabbro, Griffiths, and Gradisar, 2011; Suler, 1999; Ko, Yen, Yen, Chen, and Chen, 2012). In these cases, patients are said to be "addicted *on* the Internet" as opposed to "addicted *to* the Internet." In contrast, generalized pathological Internet use (GPIU) is characterized by behaviors that can be conducted only online, such as participation in chat groups and use of Facebook, Twitter, or other social media. This distinction is important because of its implications for treatment and intervention, a topic to be explored below.

It is important to note that, at present, PIU is not recognized as a distinct psychiatric disorder within the official diagnostic system of the American Psychiatric Association, the Statistical Manual of Mental Disorders, Version 5 (DSM5, APA, 2013). When the manual was updated in 2013, the DSM scientific workgroup considering behavioral addictions came to the conclusion that the current evidence did not support PIU as a distinct addiction syndrome with severe clinical impairment and adverse social consequences (Petry et al., 2014). This puts PIU in a group of behavioral addictions, including addiction to pornography, exercise, sex, or food, that have been endorsed by some researchers and clinicians but have yet to be regarded broadly by the scientific community as psychiatric disorders. Consequently, treatments that are specifically designed for PIU, some of which are described in the following chapter, are unlikely to be covered by health insurance policies.

The DSM workgroup did find sufficient evidence to include addiction to online gaming (Internet Gaming Disorder) in the DSM5, but not as an accepted disorder. Internet Gaming Disorder was included in an appendix to DSM5 for conditions that warrant additional research and clinical experience prior to consideration for inclusion as an official disorder. Subsequent to the DSM5, an international collaboration of experts developed a proposed standardized method for assessing Internet gaming disorder consistent with the proposed DSM-5 definition, in the hopes that scientists would move forward together in this field in a way that would permit an accumulation and refinement of scientific knowledge (Petry et al., 2014). A similar, large-scale collaborative approach appears to be necessary for science to advance the understanding of how other problematic online activities emerge, progress, impact individuals, and resolve.

How Is PIU Measured?

Investigators have been developing instruments for measuring PIU, for both clinical and research purposes (Aboujaoude, 2010). These vary in modality, length, and intended application. While some instruments have performed well in early methodological studies (Lortie and Guitton, 2013), no single accepted standard exists. As seen in the examples shown in Table 2.1, some of the instruments were designed to be self-administered, while others were administered by a qualified interviewer and/or third-person peer rater. At least one instrument is based on archival file information alone.

Most of the instruments share a high degree of overlap in the content areas assessed. These areas include

- **preoccupation** (e.g., "When I am not online, I often think about the Internet," Davis, Flett, and Besser, 2002)
- **regulation problems** (e.g., "I find it difficult to control my Internet use," Caplan, 2000)
- **functional and social impairment** (e.g., "I am often late for appointments because I'm online when I shouldn't be," Armstrong, Phillips, and Saling, 2000; "How often do others in your life complain to you about the amount of time you spend online?", Young, 1998)
- **experiences suggesting tolerance or withdrawal** (e.g., "Do you find that you need to spend more and more time on the Internet to feel satisfied?" "Do you feel distressed when you cannot connect to the Internet?", Thatcher and Goolam, 2005).

A few instruments explore other issues, such as

- **secretive uses** (e.g., "How often do you try to hide how long you've been online?", Young, 1998)
- **the role of Internet use in distraction from daily life** (e.g., "When I am online I don't think about my responsibilities," Davis et al., 2002).

Finally, only a few of these instruments have been extensively tested to determine whether they can be used in clinical settings to identify individuals with clinically significant PIU (Caplan, 2010; Chang and Man Law, 2008; Jia and Jia, 2009). We are not aware of any studies that compare results on an assessment instrument with standardized clinical assessments of PIU.

Table 2.1. Thirteen Published Instruments Designed to Assess Problematic Internet Use

Instrument Name	Description	Application	Source of Most Recent Version of Instrument
Internet Addictive Disorder Scale	7 items interview assessment	Clinical diagnosis	Goldberg, 1996
Internet-Related Addictive Behavior Inventory	32 items; self-report survey	Research	Brenner, 1997
Pathological Internet Use Scale	13 items; self-report survey	Research	Morahan-Martin et al., 1997
Chinese Internet Addiction Scale	28 items; self-report survey	Research screen	Chen et al., 1999
Internet Related Problems Scale	20 items; self-report survey	Research screen	Armstrong et al., 2000
Online Cognition Scale	36 items; self-report survey	Clinical and job screen	Davis et al., 2002
Internet Addiction Test (IAT)	20 items; survey or interview assessment	Research and clinical screen	Young, 1998
Structured Interview	72+ items; interview assessment	Clinical screen	Beard, 2005
Problematic Internet Use Questionnaire	20 items; self-report survey	Research screen	Thatcher et al., 2005
Problematic Internet Usage Scale	59 items; self-report survey	Research screen	Ceyhan et al., 2007
Index of Problematic Online Experiences	26 items; self-report survey	Research and clinical screen	Mitchell et al., 2009
Compulsive Internet Use Scale	14 items; self-report survey	Research and clinical	Meerkerk et al., 2009
Generalized Problematic Internet Use Scale 2	15 items; self-report survey	Research	Caplan, 2010

How Common Is PIU?

Reviews of the literature report such wide variation across studies in the prevalence of PIU that the studies are not helpful in assessing the true size of the problem. For instance, a systematic review of studies of PIU among adolescents in the United States reports a range of prevalence estimates of 0 percent to 26 percent (Moreno, 2011). There are two major methodological reasons for this wide range. First, as noted above, there are multiple methods for defining and measuring PIU and no agreed-upon criteria for defining a threshold between PIU and normal (nonproblematic) Internet use. Studies that use one approach are not comparable to studies using other approaches. Second, the vast majority of studies of PIU are not conducted in representative samples with well-defined population targets. For instance, many studies are conducted in small convenience samples of college students at a single location (Moreno, 2011).

While these studies can provide some valuable information on the relationship between PIU and other psychological characteristics, they cannot provide estimates of the prevalence of PIU in the general adult population in the United States. Furthermore, because of the rapidly expanding role of the Internet in everyday life, estimates of the prevalence of PIU likely vary depending on when the studies were conducted. Studies conducted just a few years ago may underestimate the current prevalence of PIU because Internet use itself has become so much more pervasive in the past few years (Pew, 2014b). Indeed, the always-on Internet connections provided by smartphones have blurred the lines between online and offline activities.

We were able to identify only one study of PIU that was conducted in a sample representative of the U.S. general population (Aboujaoude, 2006). This study, conducted in 2004, was based on a sample of 2,513 adults (18 and over) selected via random digit dialing to household landlines. In that study, 12.3 percent of respondents reported attempts to cut back on their Internet use, and 12.4 percent reported staying online longer than intended "often" or "very often" (Aboujaoude, 2006). Smaller but still significant proportions reported that their relationships suffered as a result of their excessive Internet use (5.9 percent) and that they felt preoccupied by the Internet when offline (3.7 percent). When the authors applied diagnostic criteria proposed in the literature for PIU to this study's results, the prevalence of PIU was 0.7 percent using the most liberal set of criteria. When additional symptoms were included as criteria, the prevalence was lower (between 0.4 and 0.3 percent). In the decade since this study was conducted, Internet use has grown even more common because of the introduction of tablet computers, the increasing adoption of smartphones, the rapid expansion of social media and apps for online gaming, and the increased adoption of broadband connections at home (Pew 2014a, 2014b).

Evidence specific to the Air Force population is available from a recent RAND study, which assessed PIU in a sample of 3,479 Airmen (Miller, Martin, Yeung, Trujillo, and Timmer, 2014). The RAND study assessed PIU using the Generalized Problematic Internet Use Scale, version 2 (GPIUS2). PIU was defined using a scale score based on responses to items in five domains: (1) preference for online (vs. face-to-face) communication, (2) use of the Internet to regulate mood, (3) preoccupation with Internet use, (4) compulsive Internet use, and (5) adverse consequences of Internet use. The study found that 6 percent of Airmen scored on the negative end of the GPIUS2 (Miller, Martin, Yeung, Trujillo, and Timmer, 2014, p. 30). Given a total Air Force military population of 504,414 individuals in February 2012, if these survey results can be generalized, then more than 30,000 Airmen may be struggling with PIU. On this survey, PIU was significantly correlated with poor self-rated mental health, depressed mood, and loneliness.

What Factors Are Associated with PIU?

Although large-scale population-based studies of PIU are required to systematically examine risk factors, some common characteristics of clinical cases have been identified in the existing research literature. In one detailed review, Kuss and colleagues (2013) report that individuals with PIU tend to be disproportionately young, single adult males of Asian descent with financial problems. However, different types of PIU may be associated with different patient characteristics. For example, a Canadian case control study of problematic Internet gamblers, which recruited participants using random telephone digit dialing, described this clinical population as predominantly married men in their 40s (Wood and Williams, 2011). In contrast, studies of gaming tend to find higher prevalence among adolescents (Jackson, 2011). PIU has been associated with several social, psychological, and biological factors, shown in Table 2.2.

Table 2.2. Factors Associated with Problematic Internet Use

Factor	Source
Life stressors (e.g. family conflict)	Cotten, Goldner, Hale, and Drentea, 2011; Kuss et al., 2014; Young, 1999
Comorbid mental health conditions (particularly depression and anxiety spectrum disorders)	Cuhadar 2012; Ko et al., 2012; Shapira et al., 2003; King et al., 2011; Kuss et al., 2013; Weinstein and Lejoyeux, 2010; Caplan, 2007
Low self-esteem and social self-efficacy	Iskender and Akin, 2009
Attention deficit hyperactivity disorder (ADHD)	Ko, Yen, Chen, Yeh, and Yen, 2009; Yen, Ko, Yen, Wu, and Yang, 2007)
Behavioral problems (e.g., substance dependence and suicidal conduct)	Ko et al., 2012; Kuss et al., 2013; Kim, Ryu, Chon, Yeun, Choi, Seo, and Nam, 2006; Messias, Castro, Saini, Usman, and Peeles, 2011; Lin, Ko, Chang, Liu, Wang, Lin, Huang, Yeh, Chou, and Yen, 2014
Loneliness, social anxiety, social skills deficits	Caplan, 2010; Caplan and High, 2007; Caplan, 2005; Caplan, 2003

One study surveyed over 2,700 Singaporean youth ages 12 to 18 and found that respondents who spent more than five hours a day online were significantly more likely, relative to their peers who spent less time online, to have reported initiating Internet activity prior to age seven, to live in households with no rules regarding Internet surfing, not to have someone they felt like they could confide in, and to feel sad or depressed (Mythily, Qiu, and Winslow, 2008). Neuroimaging studies have shown that individuals experiencing gaming urges generate brain responses that overlap with those associated with drug cravings found in individuals with substance dependencies (Ko, Liu, Hsiao, Yen, Yang, Lin, Yen, and Chen, 2009). Some of the brain areas observed have also been associated with general reward sensitivity in a separate sample (Dong, Huang, and Du, 2011; see, also, Lortie et al., 2013).

The causal relationship between these factors and PIU is largely undetermined. One recognized hypothesis states that those with preexisting psychological and social problems are most vulnerable to PIU (Kraut, Kiesler, Boneya, Cummings, Helgeson, and Crawford, 2002). However, most of the studies showing such relationships have examined correlations in cross-sectional data, so that it was not possible to distinguish whether the risk factor occurred prior to the development of PIU. One notable exception is a study by Ko and colleagues (2009), which employed a two-year prospective follow-up design and found that ADHD, social phobia, and a measure of trait hostility significantly predicted subsequent PIU among Chinese adolescents (see also Ko, Yen, Yen, Lin, and Yang, 2007). Additional longitudinal research is greatly needed to supplement these findings. In addition, cross-cultural variations in the predictors of PIU have yet to be examined.

What Are the Consequences of PIU?

Several studies have identified adverse functional and psychosocial consequences associated with PIU. Functional consequences include self-reported problems with time management, sleep, motivation, finances, and job performance (Kuss et al., 2013; Weinstein and Lejoyeux, 2010; Young, 2004). Absenteeism has also been cited as a negative consequence of PIU, as well as "presenteeism," being present but not performing at full capacity (Austin and Totaro, 2011). As such, it's not surprising that we also see some evidence of a drop in official and self-reported grades in children and adolescents (Jackson, Von Eye, Fitzgerald, Witt, and Zhao, 2011; Lin, Ko, and Wu, 2011; Mythily et al., 2008).

According to a variety of surveys among academic and clinical samples, as well as clinical observations, psychosocial consequences of PIU include increased social withdrawal, relationship problems, victimization, disclosure of private information, and emotion regulation difficulties (Kraut, Patterson, Lundmark, Kiesler, Mukopadhyay, and Scherlis, 1998; Kuss et al., 2013; Lin et al., 2011). There is also some evidence of increased aggressiveness associated with excessive use of violent video games (Ivory and Kalyanaraman, 2007; Saleem, Anderson, and Gentile, 2012) and increases in sexually transmitted infections among those using the Internet to find new sexual partners (Kubicek, Carpineto, McDavitt, Weiss, and Kipke. 2011).

An Integrated Model of PIU

Figure 2.1. Davis's Cognitive-Behavioral Model of PIU

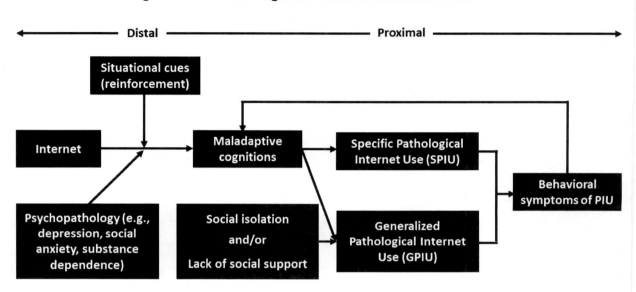

SOURCE: Davis, 2001, p. 190.

Figure 2.1 shows the cognitive-behavioral model of PIU, which integrates current knowledge about the risk factors, psychological processes, and consequences of PIU (Davis, 2001). The model is based on the diathesis-stress model, where an individual has a predisposed vulnerability (psychopathology) that can combine with situational cues (in this case, access to the Internet along with potential life stressors) to result in abnormal behavior. The rapid gratification offered on the Internet can be reinforcing, be it from the pleasure of looking at online pornography or the thrill associated with winning at an online game. The person can be conditioned to seek these rewards again in the presence of situational cues, such as a computer screen or an emotional reminder of how pleasurable his or her last Internet session was. This keeps vulnerable individuals coming back for more use of the Internet, because it continually provides pleasure or relief from some underlying psychopathology (like depression or social anxiety in face-to-face situation).

Maladaptive cognitions are the central feature; a person begins to have negative thoughts like "I am worthless offline, but I am someone online," or "The Internet is my only friend; everyone treats me badly offline." These directly lead to either specific pathological Internet use (SPIU) or generalized pathological Internet use (GPIU), as defined above. According to the cognitive-behavioral model, GPIU may be more likely than SPIU to result from social isolation and/or lack of support from family and friends.

Finally, behavioral symptoms emerge that can lead to discovery by oneself or others that use is problematic. These are directly linked to maladaptive thoughts, such as obsessive thoughts about using the Internet, thoughts that the Internet is one's only friend, and considerable distress when not online (for example, "what am I missing?"). Use of the Internet can also be problematic as it interferes with one's daily routine and activities and leads to continued isolation from others or unhealthy feelings (for example, guilt about too much use and shame from trying to hide use), which continues the cycle.

The cognitive-behavioral model has been used in the research literature to inform intervention approaches targeted at reducing the behavioral problems resulting from PIU. Primarily, the model has been used to inform interventions that target the maladaptive cognitions influencing both GPIU and SPIU. We review the concept of cognitive-behavioral therapies and the research on the approach in Chapter Three.

Conclusion

At present the literature on PIU is mixed on some basic scientific questions. On the one hand, the phenomenon of PIU, of individuals who have serious difficulty controlling their own Internet use, is widely recognized. PIU is not controversial as a new clinical phenomenon. On the other hand, there is considerable debate concerning the theoretical interpretation of this set of symptoms. In particular, there is debate regarding whether the symptoms of PIU represent a completely new psychiatric disorder or these symptoms should instead be considered components of some other underlying disorder or combination of disorders, such as major depression or attention deficit hyperactivity disorder. The evidence is quite strong that people with PIU are likely to have one or more of these other disorders. At this point in time, PIU is best considered a pattern of behavioral and cognitive symptoms which may present distinct operational challenges for the Air Force, as many Airmen require access to the Internet in the course of their everyday work and personal lives. PIU has important clinical implications, because it may be a common behavioral marker of significant mental health problems that might go undetected or untreated but does not call for a targeted clinical response involving entirely new psychiatric treatments and resources.

The fact that PIU is still new as a mental health problem and as an area of scientific research has particular implications for the Air Force, where the age divide between senior and junior Airmen may correspond to a cultural divide with respect to patterns of Internet use. Senior commanders and mental health professionals may be largely unaware of the ways that junior Airmen have grown up using the Internet for entertainment and social purposes. Because of this gap, continued monitoring of the scientific literature on PIU is particularly important for the Air Force. There is not a single accepted definition of PIU. Most of the definitions used by researchers and clinicians are modeled on definitions of addiction: Individuals with PIU are prone to excessive and compulsive use of the Internet to the point that their everyday functioning and relationships are impaired. They develop tolerance, so they must increase their use to get the same reward, and they suffer from withdrawal-like symptoms when they cannot be online. While there is no consensus regarding the specific definitional criteria for PIU, there is wide

11

recognition that PIU occurs as a serious behavioral problem. Many think the symptoms associated with PIU reflect a disorder such as depression rather than PIU being a distinct disorder with a unique etiology. PIU is not listed as a psychiatric diagnosis in the American Psychiatric Association's official catalog of disorders, the Diagnostic and Statistical Manual of Mental Disorders, Version 5 (DSM-5).

Similarly, PIU's prevalence in the population at large is unclear, but a recent RAND study involving U.S. Air Force members shows 6 percent of young adult males—members of the first generation to come of age in an Internet-saturated environment—may have persistent difficulties controlling their online activities. For some, Internet access makes it easier to engage in gambling or viewing pornography—reinforcing activities that bring them back for more. Others turn to the Internet for social connectedness, preferring online relationships to face-to-face relationships, and still others use the Internet out of distraction.

The consequences are broad and potentially serious, including poor performance at work or school, friction with friends and family, and failure to perform normal daily tasks. A variety of associated factors have been identified, such as social withdrawal, victimization, emotional instability, aggression, anxiety and depression, substance abuse, and suicidal behavior.

Chapter Three. Prevention and Treatment Strategies

As noted in the previous chapter, PIU first came to the attention of clinicians when patients presented with the inability to control their own use of the Internet. To date, no consensus has emerged as to whether their symptoms represent an entirely new diagnosis or simply a problematic behavior pattern that is best considered using existing diagnostic categories. The development of prevention and treatment approaches to PIU reflects this emerging and still unresolved body of scientific research. Clinicians have attempted to provide treatments based on existing models of care, such as cognitive-behavioral therapy (CBT[1]), that are proven to help patients with anxiety disorders or depression. Principles of substance use treatment, including extended periods of abstinence, have also been incorporated into treatments. In this chapter we review the existing research literature on both prevention and treatment approaches that have been applied to PIU over the past two decades.

This review takes a public health approach, first examining prevention programs that can be applied to entire populations to reduce the development of PIU and, second, examining treatments that have been tested to help individuals who have developed PIU to change their behavior, reduce their distress, and mitigate the adverse consequences on their lives. In the broadest sense, prevention programs applied to the Air Force could include the entire range of policies related to Internet access for Airmen while on the job, as well as specific techniques that individuals might use to help self-regulate their Internet use. The treatments are aimed at the relatively small group of individuals for whom these prevention methods do not prove sufficient. One of the important tasks for overall policy in the Air Force is to develop a comprehensive policy that links prevention and treatment into a single coherent strategy.

Prevention Strategies

Self-Regulation

We were unable to locate any studies evaluating the use of prevention and self-regulation strategies for PIU. Nevertheless, self-regulation strategies are a major part of multi-component

---

[1] Cognitive-behavioral therapy (CBT) is a short-term, structured psychotherapy that focuses on identifying and modifying unhelpful or maladaptive thoughts and behaviors through the use of collaborative techniques and independent practices, such as thought restructuring, goal setting, and behavioral "homework" assignments outside therapy sessions. It was first developed in the early 1960s for treatment of depression by Aaron Beck and has since been adapted to treat a variety of mental health disorders and behavioral concerns from anxiety and depression to substance use disorders and pathological gambling (Beck, 2011).

cognitive-behavioral interventions for PIU, which are reviewed in greater detail below (Young, 2010). These strategies include self-monitoring use, committing to self or others to limit use, and rewarding oneself for meeting goals of limited use.

Self-regulation refers to strategies that individuals, family members, and workplaces can use to help individuals control their own Internet use either before it develops into PIU or after a problem has developed. For instance, self-regulation methods include motivational components, system involvement to block usage (e.g., blocking access to particular websites), and educational components to inform the public about what signs to look for regarding their own or others' use (Larose, Mastro, and Eastin, 2001; Foundation, 1999). These strategies to control PIU may be somewhat difficult for the individual unless there is a strong level of motivation to change. As with other behavioral addictions, individuals not considering change or unaware they have a problem may have a hard time self-regulating their use without help (Prochaska and DiClemente, 2005). It is possible that with motivation to change behavior or even awareness of the nature of the problem, individuals may recognize the problematic nature of their own behavior and self-regulate their usage before it reaches the extremes, and tools exist to support that endeavor.

Self-regulation is cited as an essential component of any treatment plan for PIU, particularly if the individual needs to use the Internet for work, scheduling, and connection with family/friends. For example, a lawyer who uses the Internet daily for work but who struggles with visiting pornographic websites would need to learn strategies to regulate use of the specific websites associated with the problem. Self-regulation strategies have been likened to weight-loss programs, where the individual still needs sustenance but must regulate caloric intake and be more selective about the foods consumed (Young and de Abreu, 2011).

There are multiple online tools available, for purchase and free of charge, to assist with prevention and self-regulation; they can be downloaded by an individual, family, or a workplace/institution. Some examples are presented in Table 3.1. These tools can block access to websites specified by the user, limit usage of time-consuming websites (e.g., limiting access to Facebook to a specific number of minutes per day before access is restricted), or provide personal time and usage statistics for the user to determine how much time is spent on certain websites per day. Assessments based on validated PIU scales like the Internet Addiction Test (IAT) and tips for self-regulation strategies are also available online.

Table 3.1. Examples of Online Resources of Self-Regulation Strategies

Type of Resource	Source	Web Address
Self-regulation information	Helpguide.org	http://www.helpguide.org/mental/internet_cybersex_addiction.htm
	University of Texas at Austin Counseling and Mental Health Center	http://cmhc.utexas.edu/internetuse.html#selfhelp
	Texas State University Counseling Center	http://www.counseling.txstate.edu/resources/shoverview/bro/interadd.html
Self-administered tests for Internet addiction	Internet Addiction Test	http://netaddiction.com/internet-addiction-test/
	Partners of Internet Addicts Test	http://netaddiction.com/partners-of-internet-addict-test/
	Parent-Child Internet Addiction Test	http://netaddiction.com/parent-child-internet-addiction-test/
	Video and Online Game Addiction Test	http://netaddiction.com/are-you-an-obsessive-online-gamer/
	Online Sex Addiction Test	http://netaddiction.com/cybersex-self-test/
	Internet Gambling Addiction Test	http://netaddiction.com/are-you-a-compulsive-online-gambler/
	Auction Addiction Test	http://netaddiction.com/are-you-addicted-to-ebay-or-other-online-auctions/
Tools to monitor or limit Internet use	Freedom	http://macfreedom.com/
	Anti-social	http://anti-social.cc/
	Rescue Time	https://www.rescuetime.com/

Workplace Internet Policies

Most companies and employers in the United States have policies and practices in place to monitor employee Internet use (American Management Association, 2008). The majority of the research on workplace Internet policies discusses practices by employers to limit or block Internet usage at work to prevent a decrease in productivity. For instance, companies may track employee Internet usage on a daily or weekly basis by logging Internet chat conversations, monitoring web activity during work hours or from work computers, capturing screen shots when employees visit restricted sites, and keystroke monitoring. There are also psychologically informed policies for regulating Internet use within the workplace; however, limiting use is complex and based on the unique needs of the company and its workers (Gumbus and Grodzinsky, 2006). There are two types of policies typically employed for reducing Internet use at work: proactive policies that establish rules up front for all employees (e.g., no use of specific websites during work hours), and reactive policies that respond to productivity issues related to few restrictions on Internet use (Grodzinsky and Gumbus, 2005).

With the main goal of increasing productivity during work hours, employers try to find balance between monitoring Internet use and frustrating employees to the point of dissatisfaction with the policies (Stanton and Weiss, 2000; Urbaczewski and Jessup, 2002). Employers also must identify what is meant by appropriate personal use of the Internet on work-related equipment and time. For example, does the employer tolerate some use of the Internet for personal reasons (e.g., checking bus schedules, reading newspaper on lunch break) or does it completely block certain websites during work hours? Issues may come up if employees need to access blocked websites for work purposes (e.g., to research a topic for an upcoming report). Policies can typically be enacted through information technology (IT) departments, with clear rules established and posted so employees are aware of the restrictions and appropriateness of personal use.

Cyberwellness Prevention Programs

Employers have traditionally responded to violations of Internet policies with discipline or termination. Few companies (approximately 2 percent) report use of rehabilitation programs if PIU is identified (Young and Case, 2004). Recent commentary has brought attention to the potential for companies to be held liable for imposing sanctions on employees for PIU when the company itself has provided the employee access to the Internet (Kakabadse, Porter, and Vance, 2009; Young, 2010). This may be one reason some companies have begun to develop "cyberwellness" programs to teach employees about the safe and appropriate use of the Internet. These corporate training programs are similar to sensitivity training for sexual harassment or diversity training, which are designed to grow employee awareness of issues, reduce occurrence of incidents, and decrease liabilities (Young, 2010). Employers rate these trainings, combined with development and enforcement of Internet use policies, as effective in making employees aware of Internet use policies (Young and Case, 2004), but we found no empirical evidence suggesting these programs have been effective at reducing PIU. It has been suggested that employee assistance programs can assist with referral to treatment, but employers must weigh the costs and benefits (e.g., potential litigation, need to hire and train someone new, financial impact on company) associated with termination versus rehabilitation (Young, 2010).

Treatment Strategies

Overview of Treatment Studies

We located ten reviews of PIU since 2008 that included an empirical review of PIU treatment (King et al., 2011; Winkler et al., 2013; Kuss et al., 2013; Khazaal et al., 2012; Liu, Liao and

Smith, 2012; Kaneez et al., 2013; Aboujaoude, 2010; Cash et al., 2012; Shaw and Black, 2008; Petersen et al., 2009; Huang, Li, and Tao, 2010). These review studies have typically focused on psychological treatments, probably because there are very few published pharmacological studies in the literature. The reviews generally conclude that more research is needed before conclusions or recommendations can be proposed. Randomized controlled trials of PIU treatments, the gold standard in psychological and pharmacological fields for demonstrating efficacy of a treatment, remain rare. Limitations of the reviewed studies point to inconsistent definitions and assessments of PIU, which raises concerns about the comparability of the clinical work conducted in this area. Procedures for the studies themselves are limited by lack of randomization to treatment groups, lack of control groups, and lack of any comparison groups in the majority of studies. In addition, most of the studies have small sample sizes and lack detailed specification of the treatment procedures. Most notably, the majority of studies fail to meet guidelines necessary for evaluating quality of clinical trials (King et al., 2011; Liu, Liao, and Smith, 2012), limiting the generalizability and interpretability of the findings. Still, despite notable limitations, the literature base for PIU treatment is growing and can inform future research and clinical efforts with adults and adolescents. In the sections that follow, we review the available randomized controlled trials, case-control studies, case reports, and pre-post studies (i.e., preexperimental design) related to psychological treatment and pharmacological treatment of PIU. We briefly discuss the potential for support groups in the PIU arena. Lastly, we briefly describe the inpatient and outpatient PIU centers we were able to locate in the United States and abroad.

One issue that cuts across the specific treatment approaches is whether treatment should focus on abstinence or harm reduction. *Abstinence* refers to completely stopping use, which can be very helpful for recovering from drugs and alcohol. *Harm reduction* involves reducing or limiting use (such as use only at night after activities are completed; checking Facebook once per day; playing games for two hours after homework is complete; not visiting pornographic websites while at work) to avoid the negative consequences associated with excessive and problematic Internet use. Researchers have argued that harm reduction approaches may be most appropriate for treating PIU (Khazaal et al., 2012; Orzack and Orzack, 1999; Young and de Abreu, 2011), and with few exceptions, the majority of treatment strategies focus on continued harm reduction, often after a period of temporary abstinence. It should be noted we found no empirical evidence to support one philosophy over the other in regard to lasting treatment outcomes. Still, for many individuals, use of a computer with Internet access is essential for work and communication with family and friends, making complete abstinence difficult. This is one reason the harm reduction approach may be more attractive than abstinence-based treatment programs.

Psychological Interventions

Cognitive-Behavioral Therapy

Cognitive-behavioral therapy (CBT) has been effective in many areas of psychopathology, from depression and anxiety to disorders like pathological gambling and substance abuse (Pallesen et al., 2005; McHugh, Hearon and Otto, 2010; Butler et al., 2006; Olatunji, Cisler, and Deacon, 2010). CBT targets both maladaptive thoughts and problematic behaviors. In the example of substance use disorders, CBT is used to identify triggers related to thoughts ("I cannot make it through the day without a drink"), feelings (feeling anxious in public and using marijuana to numb out), and behaviors (walking by the street corner every day where a drug dealer hangs out). The individual learns alternative coping strategies like modifying thoughts ("I can call my sponsor if I get overwhelmed and feel like I need a drink to make it through the day") and behaviors (learning an alternate way to get to work that doesn't pass by that street corner). He or she learns to manage difficult emotions (e.g., by using breathing techniques when anxious), self-monitoring and delayed gratification skills, and social skills like assertiveness and refusal of offers to use. Likewise, CBT for PIU has focused on monitoring maladaptive thoughts ("I am no one if I'm not online"), understanding affective and situational triggers (loneliness, need to escape from stressful life events), learning alternative coping skills, and engaging in life activities that do not revolve around Internet use (Young and de Abreu, 2011). Acknowledging that one has a problem, monitoring and documenting personal online usage, learning better time management skills, identifying the underlying causes of the problematic behavior, and finding support through family, friends, and professional resources are also components of many CBT treatments (Kaneez et al., 2013; Khazaal et al., 2012; Young, 2007; Young, 2011).

Pathological gambling has been noted in treatment studies as having a similar diagnostic structure to PIU, and there is evidence that CBT is efficacious compared to control conditions for pathological gambling, with treatment gains observed during up to 12 months of follow-up (Sylvain, Ladouceur, and Boisvert, 1997; Ladouceur et al., 2001; Fong, 2005). As the treatment literature on PIU is nascent, researchers have tended to translate efficacious CBT interventions from pathological gambling to treat PIU. This work is based on the cognitive-behavioral model, which has been modified specifically to understand PIU (Davis, 2001).

Review of CBT Studies

CBT for PIU is a growing area of research both in the United States and abroad with the majority of the published CBT studies conducted with non-U.S. samples of adolescents, most specifically with Chinese adolescents struggling with problems resulting from Internet gaming. A recent review of the published treatment studies in China reported that 18 of the 24 reviewed studies were CBT-based (Liu, Liao, and Smith, 2012). However, the studies are generally not of high enough quality to definitely demonstrate treatment efficacy. The review concluded that the evidence for CBT alone and CBT in combination with group therapy, military training, and/or family therapy is not conclusive but suggestive of promise in the treatment of Chinese subjects ages 9 to 23 struggling with PIU. Though few studies compare CBT to control groups, at least one RCT has been conducted to examine the effect of CBT on excessive gaming among Chinese male adolescents (Li and Dai, 2009). Results from this study demonstrated promise of the 12 individual biweekly CBT sessions on reducing negative cognitions associated with PIU compared to an active therapy control group, but both CBT and the comparative basic counseling approach similarly led to reductions in PIU. It is also important to consider the generalizability of these results to the Air Force population, which is culturally and socially much different from the groups treated in these studies. While these studies may demonstrate the promise of treatments that are based on CBT principles, the specific techniques are likely to need extensive adaptation to Airmen.

Though research on the adult treatment of PIU is lacking, at least two studies report preexperimental designs in this population. In the first study, conducted at Inpatient Treatment at the Center for Internet Addiction in Bradford, Pennsylvania (Young, 2007; Young, 2013), two samples were both treated with CBT for Internet addiction (CBT-IA) (Young, 2011), with positive findings on improved control of use, motivation to limit use, and better time management for up to six months of postintervention follow-up. In a treatment follow-up study of Chinese young adults (Ge et al., 2011), the treated sample demonstrated improvement relative to controls in attention and cognitive functioning at three months post–group CBT, as measured by event-related potentials. No behavioral outcomes (e.g., reduced time spent on the Internet) were reported. In addition to these studies, there are also published case studies detailing the use of CBT with individual American and Greek patients (Hall and Parsons, 2001; Lee, 2011; Siomos et al., 2010b), and papers and chapters describing CBT protocols without presentation of outcomes in German, Dutch, and American treatment centers (Jager et al., 2012; Rooij et al., 2012; Wölfling, Müller, and Beutel, 2012; Young, 1999).

CBT Combined with Other Psychological and Pharmacological Treatments

Similar to studies of CBT alone, studies that combine CBT approaches with other treatments (e.g., medications, electro-acupuncture) appear promising but are primarily based on non-U.S. samples with adolescents. The two randomized controlled trials available examined Chinese and Korean adolescents. One of these studies found the combination of CBT and bupropion, an anti-depressant medication which is also used to treat nicotine addiction, to have a statistically significant benefit over treatment with medication only among a sample of 65 Korean adolescents suffering from excessive online game play and comorbid major depressive disorder (Kim et al., 2012). The combination of CBT and medication has also been found to be superior to one of the methods alone in treatment of depression for adolescents and adults (Pampallona et al., 2004; Vitiello, 2009), indicating that the use of CBT for PIU may have an additive component for treatment success over medication alone. The other randomized controlled trial of a combination treatment was with Chinese adolescents ages 12–17. This study tested an intervention which combined eight sessions of group CBT with training related to PIU for both parents and teachers (Du, Jiang, and Vance, 2010). A control sample received no intervention for PIU. PIU symptoms declined in both groups over the six month follow-up period, but the intervention group had statistically significant reduction in symptoms relative to the control group. Students in the intervention group reported significantly better control of time, fewer conduct problems and emotional symptoms, and increased positive social behaviors. Thus, with Asian adolescents, the use of CBT enhanced by medication or family/teacher components appears efficacious compared to control.

There is little known to date regarding the combined effectiveness of CBT with other therapeutic approaches. For example, some research has examined the effects of CBT combined with electro-acupuncture (a treatment which combines traditional acupuncture needles with mild electrical stimulation) in adult PIU patients, but the relative contributions of these two strategies were not experimentally investigated. That is, though CBT with electro-acupuncture appears efficacious, it is unclear whether the electro-acupuncture is a necessary adjunctive method for CBT efficacy or if CBT functions better alone than when combined with the method (Zhu et al., 2008; Zhu et al., 2011; Zhu et al., 2012). In addition, researchers at the Computer Addiction Study Center at the McLean Hospital in Belmont, Massachusetts, combined group CBT and motivational interviewing components to treat middle-aged men with problematic Internet sexual behavior (Orzack et al., 2006). While the 16-week group sessions helped reduce depression and increase quality of life for the 35 patients enrolled in the study, there was no observable change to Internet sexual behavior posttreatment. Finally, a qualitative review of a CBT with motivational interviewing treatment protocol for 12 patients in a Dutch treatment center indicated therapists reported the treatment was effective and appropriate with PIU patients (Rooij et al., 2012). While patients generally reported satisfaction and appropriateness of approach, no outcomes were reported to evaluate effects of the program on PIU.

CBT remains a promising approach to the treatment of patients with PIU, both on theoretical grounds and because of the demonstrated efficacy of CBT for conditions that commonly co-occur and may underlie many cases of PIU. However, the limitations of the existing literature, including small sample sizes and uncontrolled study designs, do not support definitive statements about its efficacy, when used either alone or in combination with other psychological (e.g., family therapy), pharmacological (e.g., selective serotonin reuptake inhibitors), and electro-acupuncture methods.

Other Psychological Interventions

Although CBT is by far the most researched and utilized treatment approach for PIU, other studies have discussed non-CBT treatments with promising results. Notably, researchers have used an online personalized feedback approach, acceptance and commitment therapy (ACT) and reality therapy (RT), multimodal treatments without CBT components, and promotion of exercise routines. Researchers designed a pilot RCT with Chinese university students to examine the efficacy of the Healthy Online Self-Helping Center (HOSC), an online self-help program based on Motivational Interviewing, client-centered communication style, personalized feedback, and goal setting (Su et al., 2011). HOSC was more effective than the control in reducing online hours per week and PIU symptoms, demonstrating improved online satisfaction at one-month follow-up. The clinical intervention ACT, which helps patients focus on living according to their values and setting behavioral goals, was used in one study with six adult males to treat problematic Internet pornography viewing (Twohig and Crosby, 2010). Reductions in Internet pornography viewing were observed after eight sessions, with improvements still apparent at the three-month follow-up. Researchers also used group-based RT, which helps patients focus on making behavioral changes and goals in spite of negative emotions, in an RCT with 25 Korean university students struggling with PIU (Kim, 2008). Compared to control, RT patients reduced PIU symptoms and reported increased self-esteem after ten biweekly group sessions, though long-term postintervention is unknown. Multimodal counseling with group, family, and individual counseling combined with case work was successful in reducing PIU symptoms, but not in increasing psychological well-being as targeted among a primarily male sample of 56 Chinese adolescents (Shek, Tang, and Lo, 2009). Lastly, one of the more common approaches used by Chinese researchers is exercise prescriptions (e.g., regimented exercise routines), though there is no clear evidence for the efficacy of these approaches alone or combined with other treatments like CBT (Liu, Liao, and Smith, 2012).

Pharmacological Interventions

Pharmacological treatments for PIU are also being studied but are in the early stages of establishing efficacy. RCTs in other areas of behavioral addictions and impulse control disorders (e.g., pathological gambling) suggest medications have promise for PIU (Aboujaoude, 2010), but few conclusions or recommendations can be drawn from the pharmacological studies. Nevertheless, noncontrolled studies and case reports cite preliminary evidence for use of pharmacological treatments for PIU, primarily for Internet gaming and excessive pornography viewing. Case reports with young adults cite successful single-case use of selective serotonin reuptake inhibitors (SSRIs) (Atmaca, 2007) and naltrexone (Bostwick and Bucci, 2008), the latter being a main medication used to treat cravings among those with substance use disorders. Evidence from a ten-week, open-label trial of an SSRI followed by a nine-week, double-blind, placebo-controlled discontinuation phase reported reductions in Internet usage time per week by half among 14 adult subjects with impulsive-compulsive Internet usage disorder (Dell'Osso et al., 2008). Other small observational studies have shown promise of a psychostimulant treating 62 Korean children with attention deficit disorder and excessive Internet video game playing (Han et al., 2009) and an antidepressant medication to reduce cravings to play Internet games among 11 Korean adolescents (Han, Hwang, and Renshaw, 2010). Randomized controlled studies that would provide stronger evidence of treatment efficacy have not been reported.

Support Groups

Support groups stemming from 12-step philosophies have been helpful in recovery of behavioral addictions such as substance use disorders and pathological gambling. For example, both Alcoholics Anonymous (AA) and Narcotics Anonymous (NA) have empirical support for their effectiveness in helping individuals abstain from alcohol and drugs (Kaskutas, 2009; Laudet, 2008). In addition, Gamblers Anonymous, a 12-step support group approach adapted from AA, has also been shown to be efficacious when completed alone or as an adjunct to CBT (Fong, 2005; Petry, 2005).

Experts in PIU suggest that attendance at these groups has the potential to help individuals with PIU (Young, 1999; Chrismore, 2011). They encourage attendance at groups focused on substance abuse and gambling as well as at Emotions Anonymous, which is a nonspecific support group focused on recovery from emotional difficulties. While there are reports of support groups specifically designed for PIU (Saisan et al., 2013), we were unable to locate any through an online search.

Online support groups may be more easily accessible, but caution may be needed. First, this modality can facilitate exposure to problematic online activities. Second, since PIU is associated with detriments in face-to-face interactions (Caplan and High, 2007), online support groups could potentially limit opportunities for face-to-face socialization compared to community-based treatment.

Specialized Outpatient and Inpatient Treatment Centers

Through an Internet-based search and discussions with experts in the field, we located six specialized treatment centers in the United States, Greece, China, and Korea. The three American centers are Inpatient Treatment at the Center for Internet Addiction, Bradford, Pennsylvania (Kimberly S. Young, Director), the outpatient Computer Addiction Study Center at the McLean Hospital in Belmont, Massachusetts (Maressa H. Orzak, Director), and the inpatient reSTART: Internet Addiction Recovery program in Fall City, Washington (co-directors Cosette Rae and Hilarie Cash). The first two focus on CBT treatment of adult PIU, with the reSTART program focusing on upwards of 20 different intervention types (e.g., CBT, mindfulness, animal-assisted therapy) in an individualized holistic approach during the 45- to 90-day inpatient stay. The Specialized Outpatient Unit for Internet and PC Addiction, based in the Department of Child and Adolescent Psychiatry of the Hippokration General Hospital of Thessaloniki in Greece, treats adolescent PIU with a focus on CBT for online gaming addiction. The Center for Internet Addiction Prevention and Counseling in South Korea has been open since 2002 and targets PIU among adolescents. Lastly, the Internet Addiction Center in Beijing, China, has received recent media attention for its intensive, military boot camp–style approach to treating adolescent PIU primarily related to excessive online gaming (Billington, 2014; Jiang, 2009). Of these centers, we were able to find published descriptions and evidence of promise for the treatment approaches utilized by the Center for Internet Addiction (Young, 2007; Young, 2011; Young, 2013) and Specialized Outpatient Unit for Internet and PC Addiction (Siomos et al., 2010a), while the Computer Addiction Study Center reported promise of mood improvements but not PIU (Orzack et al., 2006). The ReSTART program has cited unpublished outcome data on 19 adults (Cash et al., 2012), though we were not able to locate a published peer-reviewed manuscript of the findings. Not much is known about the centers in China and South Korea beyond what has been reported in the media.

Trainings for Providers in PIU Treatment Strategies

Treatment of PIU appears to be a specialized field, though the experts in the field generally suggest modified CBT for behavioral addictions like pathological gambling can be appropriate (Young and de Abreu, 2011). Training and continuing education courses are available for providers. For example, the Zur Institute offers a mostly text-based six-session, 26-credit-hour, online continuing education course for community providers, based primarily in CBT-IA and the work from the Inpatient Treatment at the Center for Internet Addiction. Additionally, in South Korea, where PIU is recognized as a national health problem, there is a focus on continuing education and counselor training. For example, the Center for Internet Addiction Prevention and Counseling in South Korea offers continuing education credits for counselors in the community, and in 2001 more than 1,000 South Korean counselors had received Internet addiction training certificates from the center (Kwon, 2007). Little is known about trainings and continuing education for counselors in China. Overall, research is needed to understand how these trainings are effective for providers not affiliated with the specialized training centers described above and how the research-based protocols (e.g., CBT-IA) are effectively implemented in the community by these providers.

Applicability of Internet-Based Treatment Approaches

Online treatment approaches are becoming an increasingly popular method to deliver informational programs, stand-alone interventions, and adjunct treatments for a variety of mental health problems such as depression and heavy alcohol use (Griffiths, Farrer, and Christensen, 2010; Ybarra and Eaton, 2005; Pull, 2006; Tait and Christensen, 2010; Lal and Adair, 2014). For example, the Internet has been used to provide education and treatment for service members and veterans reporting behavioral health concerns like posttraumatic stress disorder and hazardous alcohol use (Brief et al., 2013; Pemberton et al., 2011; Williams et al., 2009).

On one hand, these approaches might facilitate access to problematic activities among PIU patients. For example, research indicates that people with underlying psychological problems (e.g., depression, social anxiety), poor social skills, and introverted personality traits tend to be drawn to the Internet for social interaction (Davis, 2001; Caplan and High, 2007) and, thus, may miss out on the important interpersonal connection they may have in a face-to-face therapeutic or support group environment. Also, treating PIU through the mechanism facilitating the problem (i.e., the Internet) may have implications for further problems and isolation.

On the other hand, online outreach may serve as an effective first point of contact for this population. Internet programs have the ability to reach a widespread audience, can be less expensive than more intensive programs, require less staffing and expertise, can be accessed at all hours, and can provide services for individuals who might have never otherwise engaged in such care. For individuals suffering from PIU, the risks of social withdrawal and resistance to treatment may present barriers to accessing care. This may be particularly concerning for military populations due to fear of repercussions (Warner et al., 2011) and stigma associated with seeking behavioral health care (Hoge et al., 2004; Pietrzak et al., 2009; Schell and Marshall, 2008; Vogt, 2011). The use of Internet-based outreach and treatment of PIU could help surmount these barriers, though additional research is needed to support these claims.

Conclusion

As with the scientific literature on PIU in general, the literature on prevention and treatment of PIU reviewed in this chapter is limited in scope and has major gaps that remain to be filled. The literature documents a history of thoughtful, theory-guided innovation by clinicians building on solid foundations of proven treatments to apply them to a newly emerging condition. Most of the studies are small "proof of concept" studies, which have yet to be followed up with larger, more robust controlled clinical trials. Many of the studies have been conducted with samples of adolescents in East Asia, and the generalizability of the findings to the U.S. context or, more specifically, the Air Force, has not been examined. Specific treatments for PIU cannot be recommended solely on the basis of research conducted in populations so dramatically different from that of the Air Force. As of now, the literature can suggest some general strategies for preventing and treating PIU, but these strategies should be closely monitored with the understanding that they may have to be adjusted as experience is gained and new research results are generated.

Self-regulation methods, such as software programs for Internet browsers that assist the individual in controlling his or her own Internet use, are likely to be the front line of PIU prevention. One of the major reasons Internet use can be a challenge to control is the simple fact that the Internet is so accessible. Techniques that limit this accessibility may be relatively inexpensive and effective methods for preventing PIU in most people. The popularity of online software that individuals use to restrict their own access to the Internet suggests that many people experience relatively mild difficulties controlling their Internet use and might benefit from these programs. However, it is not clear how widely known or how effective these methods are in helping individuals regain control over their Internet use at a population level. Experimenting with these methods in the context of a comprehensive Internet use policy would produce valuable information. It is likely that effective prevention policies can help individuals avoid developing more serious patterns of PIU.

There is little evidence to date that PIU can or should be targeted as a uniform and distinct disorder requiring a unique treatment approach. A number of promising treatment approaches have been developed based on existing evidenced-based treatment principles, but none of the existing studies has had the rigor to truly test whether the treatment being provided affects PIU outcomes. However, that the scientific community has not isolated nor developed PIU-specific treatment does not diminish the concern for the mental health of individuals with PIU.

Evaluation of treatment recommendations for PIU should take account of the fact that many, if not most, PIU patients are likely to have comorbid psychiatric disorders for which evidence-based psychotherapeutic and pharmacological treatments do exist. (In fact, none of these treatments has disorder-specific effects.) Given that symptoms of PIU may be markers of underdiagnosed and undertreated psychiatric disorders, such as major depression or generalized anxiety disorder, Airmen who come to clinical or disciplinary attention for PIU symptoms should not be discouraged from seeking mental health services.

Thus, while the literature does not provide clear answers to the optimal strategies for PIU prevention and treatment, it does suggest that an understanding of PIU can be incorporated into existing policies and clinical practices. An important lesson for the Air Force is that PIU should be a consideration, among others, in formulating Internet use policies for the workplace. In particular, policies could include individual-level preventive interventions that promote positive self-regulation strategies. Moreover, these polices should take into account that many who chronically violate Internet use policies, despite efforts at self-control, may have more serious mental health concerns that warrant professional attention and not simply disciplinary action. With respect to treatment, the literature highlights the need for providers to be aware of the role that online activities can come to play in the lives of the people they treat, particularly young people who have grown up in an Internet-saturated environment. Providers may be unaware of the types of activities that younger Airmen engage in on the Internet, and they may lack the background to comprehend the motivations for these activities or the attraction that they hold. In most cases, clinicians will be able to provide the appropriate treatments, provided that they are aware of the need to address these behaviors and understand the underlying psychology.

Chapter Four. Implications and Recommendations

PIU remains an emerging area of science. There are some common principles guiding the definition and measurement of PIU, but no consensus on a single set of criteria. PIU is widely recognized as a behavioral pattern associated with severe functional impairment, but it is not currently recognized as an official psychiatric disorder, distinct from other established disorders. The research published to date has generally been based on convenience samples with specialized populations. Studies in representative samples are rare, and the most rigorous general population studies are already out of date given the rapidly shifting demographics of Internet use. The treatment literature is also at a relatively early stage, with studies demonstrating the acceptability of treatment among patients with PIU but no rigorous studies comparing PIU treatments against other types of mental health treatment. Nonetheless, adaptations of existing evidence-based treatments to PIU symptoms are promising.

Conclusions and Recommendations for Air Force Approaches to PIU as the Science Develops

Despite the variation in methodologies and results, some broad conclusions can be drawn. First, PIU clearly affects a nontrivial proportion of the population and involves psychosocial and functional risks. A variety of likely risk factors and consequences have been identified, such as loneliness, social anxiety, social skills deficits, victimization, emotional instability, aggressiveness, anxiety and depression, substance abuse, suicidal behavior, and performance problems at school and work. Although it remains undetermined whether PIU should be conceptualized as a distinct disorder in and of itself, related disorders such as gambling addiction may provide a useful starting point for PIU treatment research. However, although treatments based on cognitive behavioral therapy are being developed, proven, evidence-based prevention and treatment strategies that focus specifically on PIU, independent of the associated disorders, do not yet exist. Treatment research of much greater breadth and depth is needed before specific treatment, prevention, or intervention strategies can be broadly recommended to the Air Force.

Until the research on PIU matures, organizations aiming to prevent, manage, and reduce the effects of PIU can benefit from consideration of several preliminary mitigation strategies. The overall goal of these strategies is to shift the culture regarding Internet use in the Air Force so that the mental health aspects of Internet use, i.e. PIU and its common mental health comorbidities, are given appropriate priority in the operational awareness of leaders, workplace policies, and mental health treatment. Such a change in the culture of Internet use can ensure that individual Airmen who become distressed due to PIU receive the support that they need to succeed.

First, leadership can benefit from consideration of PIU in the formulation of workplace Internet use policies. Current Air Force policy recognizes the need to manage Internet use without heavily restricting access individually or across the organization in a way that would be impractical and would limit the benefits of Internet connectivity. Inappropriate use of the Internet in the workplace is recognized as a potential disciplinary issue. For instance, AFI33-129, "Transmission of Information Via the Internet," states: "Using the Internet for other than authorized purposes may result in adverse administrative or disciplinary action." Specific workplace policies and their enforcement are left to the discretion of local commanders. Consideration of the literature on PIU suggests that caution should be exercised with respect to punitive sanctions of individual Airmen for violations of Internet use policy because of the possibility of underlying mental health problems. In addition, the Air Force could avoid exacerbating the problem for Airmen with PIU by limiting exposure to Internet service to only essential tasks. Workplace Internet use policies that employ consensual monitoring, educational, prevention, and treatment services, and self-monitoring support could potentially be effective in reducing the extent, severity, and downstream consequences of PIU for the individual and the organization. As noted above, Airmen who continue to have problems controlling their Internet use, despite clear and consistently applied policies and support with self-regulation strategies, should be considered for referral to a mental health clinician.

Second, education would be useful to increase awareness of PIU at several levels within the Air Force. Although we do not recommend any stand-alone training devoted solely to the topic of PIU, organizational leadership and mental health professionals can benefit from education about the broad definition, risk factors, and negative consequences of PIU. These groups would benefit if information on the identification of PIU signs and protocols for unobtrusive mental health referral were incorporated into existing training programs. Leadership should be made aware that PIU is not just a disciplinary issue but may be an indication of a serious underlying mental health problem for which a referral to treatment may be advisable. Mental health practitioners could consider assessments for PIU, keeping in mind that there is no generally accepted measurement standard. Clinical assessments of anxiety and depressive disorders should be conducted with patients reporting PIU. This assessment might help providers detect underlying mental health problems Airmen might not have realized or felt comfortable reporting directly themselves. With respect to the education of Airmen more generally, to address the universal knowledge needs across the force, information on PIU should be inserted into existing trainings on issues related to mental health, resilience, suicide prevention, and well-being.

Third, in addition to current Air Force and DoD efforts to increase access to mental health care and reduce stigma for seeking treatment for mental health problems, these organizations can ensure that they are equipped to detect and address PIU to the greatest degree possible given the current state of the science. Ultimately, until a broader evidence base is developed to understand the mental, physical, interpersonal, and situational factors that facilitate PIU, policies that promote education and awareness, self-monitoring, and efficient and private access to wellness services represent early, exploratory steps toward successfully treating, managing, and preventing the symptoms of this potentially debilitating condition.

Finally, we recommend additional research as a cost-effective way to identify the range of organizational risks involved in PIU and efficient strategies for mitigating these risks. Both qualitative and quantitative research methods can be brought to bear.

Qualitative Exploration to Understand PIU in the Military Setting

When little is known about a phenomenon in a given setting, qualitative research methods can provide the rich, contextual information that can illuminate how that phenomenon emerges and interacts within the particular structure and culture of that setting and among that particular population. For an exploratory qualitative study of PIU in a military setting, overarching research questions of value would include

- *What does PIU in the military look like?*
    - What types of online activities tend to be associated with military personnel's PIU?
    - When does PIU tend to start? Prior to entering the military? In conjunction with other particular life events or military experiences?
    - What types of life and work-related problems do service members experience as a result of their PIU?

- *What do identification, outreach, and intervention strategies in the military look like?*
    - Do personnel with PIU recognize it as a problem, and are they willing to seek help? Are individuals coming for treatment on their own, being referred by family members, or being identified by clinicians?
    - What are obstacles to overcoming it (e.g., social pressures to interact online, mental health disorders)?
    - What understandings of PIU do military leaders and helping professionals, such as chaplains and mental health care providers, hold?
    - What strategies to identify and address PIU have service members, military leaders and helping professionals employed, and with what results?

The results of a qualitative exploration of the research questions above offer the potential to identify

- a focused set of topics appropriate for the population to be included in a large-scale survey to assess prevalence and track PIU over time
- misconceptions and counterproductive behaviors among personnel attempting to address PIU
- interest in or need for continuing education on the topic among military counselors

- contextualized examples of PIU for use in education and training materials
points of vulnerability where additional military attention or outreach may be warranted (e.g., post-divorce, post-combat, during assignments to remote locations).

Quantitative Assessment to Track Prevalence and Associated Indicators of Well-Being

Measures of PIU could be integrated into existing survey efforts to provide better estimates of the prevalence of and risk factors for PIU in the Air Force. For example, the Air Force's Community Assessment survey covers topics related to health and well-being and is conducted Air Force–wide every other year. Although survey length is always a concern, this survey is a potential opportunity to assess prevalence as well as the relationship between PIU scores and other indicators of well-being. We recommend survey items using language more broad than "Internet," as addiction-like behaviors regarding computer, smartphone and video game use more generally hold as much relevance for the military as the more narrowly focused term "Internet" implies. Otherwise, measures could underestimate the problem if respondents are not thinking of time in an online game or on their smartphones as being "on the Internet."

The Air Force could also use this survey as an opportunity to assess the extent to which the DSM-5's proposed criteria for Internet gaming disorder may be present among Airmen and whether it is associated with negative outcomes. RAND recommends that for any assessments of Internet gaming disorder, DoD adopt the proposed standardized questions reached through international collaboration (Petry et al., 2014) and publish the results so the effort can also contribute to scientific knowledge on this topic.

Conclusion

Internet connectivity provides immeasurable benefits to communication, information access, and operational efficiency to the Air Force, but it also creates an arena for problematic behavior for some individuals. While the scientific literature does not yet provide a clear clinical formulation of PIU, the evidence is clear that there is an impairing pattern of behavior involving lack of control over Internet use that is most likely to occur among people with underlying mental health concerns. There are clear steps that the Air Force can take now to expand awareness of PIU among commanders and clinicians and to incorporate this awareness into Internet use policies. Developing these policies and monitoring the continuing development of the scientific literature will enhance the Air Force's capability to manage Internet use while improving well-being among Airmen.

References

Aboujaoude, Elias, L. M. Koran, N. Gamel, M. D. Large, and R. T. Serpe, "Potential Markers For Problematic Internet Use: A Telephone Survey Of 2,513 Adults," *CNS Spectr.* Vol. 11, No.10, 2006, pp. 750–755.

Aboujaoude, Elias, "Problematic Internet Use: An Overview," *World Psychiatry,* Vol. 9, No. 2, June, 2010, pp. 85–90.

American Management Association, *Electronic Monitoring and Surveillance Survey: Over Half Of All Employers Combined Fire Workers For Email And Internet Abuse,* New York, N.Y., 2008.

American Psychiatric Association, *Diagnostic And Statistical Manual Of Mental Disorders* (5th ed.). Arlington, Va.: American Psychiatric Publishing, 2013.

Armstrong Lynette, James G. Phillips, and Lauren L. Saling, "Potential Determinants Of Heavier Internet Usage," *International Journal of Human Computational Studies,* Vol. 53, 2000, pp. 537–550.

Atmaca, Murad, "A Case Of Problematic Internet Use Successfully Treated with an SSRI-Antipsychotic Combination," *Progress in Neuro-Psychopharmacology and Biological Psychiatry,* Vol. 31, No. 4, May 9, 2007, pp. 961–962.

Austin, Wesley A., and Michael W. Totaro, "Gender Differences in the Effects of Internet Usage on High School Absenteeism," *The Journal of Socio-Economics,* Vol. 40, No. 2, 2011, pp. 192–198.

Beck, Judith S., *Cognitive Behavior Therapy* (2nd ed.), New York, N.Y.: Guilford Press, 2011.

Bertelsmann Foundation, *Self-Regulation of Internet Content*, Bielefeld, Germany: ReproZentrum Rosenberger GmbH and Co., 1999.

Billieux, Joel, and Martial Van der Linden, "Problematic Use of the Internet and Self-Regulation: A Review of the Initial Studies," *The Open Addiction Journal,* Vol. 5, 2012, pp. 24–29.

Billington, James, "China Has Secret Military-Style Camps for Internet Addicts," *New York Times*, 2014.

Bostwick, J. Michael, and Jeffrey A. Bucci, "Internet Sex Addiction Treated With Naltrexone," *Mayo Clinic Proceedings,* Vol. 83, No. 2, February, 2008, pp. 226–230.

Brief, Deborah J., Amy Rubin, Terence M. Keane, Justin L. Enggasser, Monica Roy, Eric Helmuth, John Hermos, Mark Lachowicz, Denis Rybin, and David Rosenbloom, "Web

Intervention for OEF/OIF Veterans with Problem Drinking and PTSD Symptoms: A Randomized Clinical Trial," *Journal of Consulting and Clinical Psychology,* Vol. 81, No. 5, October 2013, pp. 890–900.

Butler, A. C., J. E. Chapman, E. M. Forman, and A. T. Beck, "The Empirical Status of Cognitive-Behavioral Therapy: A Review of Meta-Analyses," *Clinical Psychology Review,* Vol. 26, No. 1, January 2006, pp. 17–31.

Byun, Sookeun, Celestino Ruffini, Juline E. Mills, Alecia C. Douglas, Mamadou Niang, Svetlana Stepchenkova, Seul Ki Lee, Jihad Loutfi, Jung-Kook Lee, Mikhail Atallah, and Marina Blanton, "Internet Addiction: Metasynthesis of 1996–2006 Quantitative Research," *CyberPsychology and Behavior,* Vol. 12, No. 2, 2009, pp. 203–207.

Caplan, Scott E., "Theory and Measurement of Generalized Problematic Internet Use: A Two-Step Approach," *Computers in Human Behavior,* Vol. 26, No. 5, September 2010, pp. 1089–1097. As of November 12, 2014:
http://www.sciencedirect.com/science/article/pii/S074756321000052X

Caplan, Scott E., and Andrew C. High, "Online Social Interaction, Psychosocial Well-Being, and Problematic Internet Use," *Internet Addiction*, John Wiley and Sons, Inc., 2007, pp. 35–53. As of November 12, 2014:
http://dx.doi.org/10.1002/9781118013991.ch3

Caplan, Scott E., "Relations Among Loneliness, Social Anxiety, and Problematic Internet Use," *CyberPsychology and Behavior*, Vol. 10, 2007, pp. 234–241.

Caplan, Scott E., "A Social Skill Account Of Problematic Internet Use," *Journal of Communication*, Vol. 55, 2005, pp. 721–736.

Caplan, Scott E., "Preference For Online Social Interaction: A Theory Of Problematic Internet Use and Psychosocial Well-Being," *Communication Research*, Vol. 30, 2003, pp.625–648.

Cash, Hilarie, Cosette D. Rae, Ann H. Steel, and Alexander Winkler, "Internet Addiction: A Brief Summary of Research and Practice," *Current Psychiatry Reviews,* Vol. 8, No. 4, November 2012, pp. 292–298.

Ceyhan, Esra, Aydogan Aykut Ceyhan, and Ayşen Gürcan, "The validity and reliability of the Problematic Internet Usage Scale," *Educational Sciences: Theory and Practice,* Vol. 7, 2007, pp. 411–416.

Chang, Man Kit, and Sally Pui Man Law, "Factor Structure For Young's Internet Addiction Test: A Confirmatory Study," *Computers in Human Behavior,* Vol. 24, No. 6, 2008, pp. 2597–2619.

Chou, Chien, Linda Condron, and John C. Belland, "A Review of the Research on Internet Addiction," *Educational Psychology Review*, Vol. 17, No. 4, 2005, pp. 363–388.

Chrismore, Shannon, Ed Betzelberger, Libby Bier, and Tonya Camacho, "Twelve-Step Recovery in Inpatient Treatment for Internet Addiction," in *Internet Addiction: A Handbook And Guide To Evaluation And Treatment*, Kimberly S. Young and Cristiano Nabuco de Abreu, eds., Hoboken, N.J.: John Wiley and Sons, Inc., 2011.

Cotten, Shelia R., Melinda Goldner, Timothy M. Hale, and Patricia Drentea, "The Importance of Type, Amount, and Timing of Internet Use for Understanding Psychological Distress," *Social Science Quarterly*, Vol. 92, No. 1, 2011, pp. 119–139.

Cuhadar, Cem, "Exploration Of Problematic Internet Use and Social Interaction Anxiety Among Turkish Pre-Service Teachers," *Computers and Education,* Vol. 59, 2012, pp. 173–181.

Davis, Richard. A., "A Cognitive-Behavioral Model Of Pathological Internet Use," *Computers in Human Behavior*, Vol. 17, 2001, pp. 187–195.

Davis, Richard. A., Gordon L. Flett, and Avi Besser, "Validation of a New Scale for Measuring Problematic Internet Use: Implications for Pre-Employment Screening," *CyberPsychology and Behavior,* Vol. 5, No. 4, 2002, pp. 331–345.

Dell'Osso, Bernardo, SallieJo Hadley, Andrea Allen, Bryann Baker, William F. Chaplin, and Eric Hollander, "Escitalopram in the Treatment of Impulsive-Compulsive Internet Usage Disorder: An Open-Label Trial Followed by a Double-Blind Discontinuation Phase," *Journal of Clinical Psychiatry,* Vol. 69, No. 3, March 2008, pp. 452–456.

Department of the Air Force, *Communications and Information Transmission of Information Via the Internet*, Air Force Communications and Information Center, Air Force Instruction 33-129, April 2001. As of November 12, 2014:
http://www.au.af.mil/au/awc/awcgate/edref/afi33-129.pdf

Dong, Guangheng, Jie Huang, and Xiaoxia Du, "Enhanced Reward Sensitivity and Decreased Loss Sensitivity in Internet Addicts: An fMRI Study During a Guessing Task," *Journal of Psychiatric Research*, Vol. 45, 2011, pp.1525–1529.

Du, Ya-song, Wenqing Jiang, and Alasdair Vance, "Longer Term Effect of Randomized, Controlled Group Cognitive Behavioural Therapy for Internet Addiction in Adolescent Students in Shanghai," *Australian and New Zealand Journal of Psychiatry,* Vol. 44, No. 2, 2010, pp. 129–134. As of November 12, 2014:
http://anp.sagepub.com/content/44/2/129.abstract

Fong, Timothy W., "Types Of Psychotherapy for Pathological Gamblers," *Psychiatry (Edgmont),* Vol. 2, No. 5, May 2005, pp. 32–39.

Gamez-Guadix, M., I. Orue, and E. Calvete, "Evaluation Of The Cognitive-Behavioral Model Of Generalized And Problematic Internet Use In Spanish Adolescents," *Psicothema,* Vol. 25, No. 3, 2013, pp. 299–306.

Ge, Ling, Xiuchun Ge, Yong Xu, Kerang Zhang, Jing Zhao, and Xin Kong, "P300 Change and Cognitive Behavioral Therapy in Subjects with Internet Addiction Disorder: A Three-Month Follow-Up Study," *Neural Regeneration Research,* Vol. 6, 2011, pp. 2037–2041.

Gray, Jennifer B., and Neal D. Gray, "The Web of Internet Dependency: Search Results for the Mental Health Professional," *International Journal of Mental Health and Addiction,* Vol. 4, 2006, pp. 307–318.

Greenfield, David N., "Psychological Characteristics Of Compulsive Internet Use: A Preliminary Analysis," *Cyberpsychology and Behavior,* Vol. 2, No. 5, 1999, pp. 403–412.

Griffiths, Kathleen M., Louise Farrer, and Helen Christensen, "The Efficacy of Internet Interventions for Depression and Anxiety Disorders: A Review of Randomised Controlled Trials," *Medical Journal of Australia,* Vol. 192, No. 11 Supplement, June 7, 2010, pp. S4–11.

Griffiths, Mark, "Internet Addiction: An Issue for Clinical Psychology?" *Clinical Psychology Forum*, Vol. 97, 1996, pp. 32–36.

Griffiths, Mark, "Internet Abuse and Internet Addiction in the Workplace," *Journal of Workplace Learning,* Vol. 22, No. 7, 2010, pp. 463–472.

Griffiths, Mark, "Sex on the Internet: Observations and Implications for Internet Sex Addiction," *Journal of Sex Research*, Vol. 38, No. 4, 2010, pp. 333–342.

Grodzinsky, Frances, and Andra Gumbus, "Internet and Productivity: Ethical Perspectives on Workplace Behavior," unpublished, 2005. As of November 12, 2014: http://biblioteca.clacso.edu.ar/ar/libros/raec/ethicomp5/docs/htm_papers/24Grodzinsky,%20Frances%20S.htm

Gumbus, Andra, and Frances S. Grodzinsky, "Ethical and Managerial Implications of Internet Monitoring," *Welch College of Business Faculty Publications,* Paper 129, 2006.

Hall, Alex S., and Jeffrey Parsons, "Internet Addiction: College Student Case Study Using Best Practices in Cognitive Behavior Therapy," *Journal of Mental Health Counseling,* Vol. 23, 2001, pp. 312–327.

Han, Doug Hyun, Jun Won Hwang, and Perry F. Renshaw, "Bupropion Sustained Release Treatment Decreases Craving for Video Games and Cue-Induced Brain Activity in Patients with Internet Video Game Addiction," *Experimental and Clinical Psychopharmacology,* Vol. 18, No. 4, August 2010, pp. 297–304.

Han, Doug Hyun, Young Sik Lee, Churl Na, Jee Young Ahn, Un Sun Chung, Melissa A. Daniels, Charlotte A. Haws, and Perry F. Renshaw, "The Effect of Methylphenidate on Internet Video Game Play in Children with Attention Deficit/Hyperactivity Disorder," *Comprehensive Psychiatry,* Vol. 50, No. 3, May–June, 2009, pp. 251–256.

Hoge, Charles W., Carl A. Castro, Stephen C. Messer, Dennis McGurk, Dave I. Cotting, and Robert L. Koffman, "Combat Duty in Iraq and Afghanistan, Mental Health Problems, and Barriers to Care," *New England Journal of Medicine*, Vol. 351, No. 1, July 1, 2004, pp. 13–22.

Huang, Xui-qin, Meng-chen Li, and Ran Tao, "Treatment of Internet Addiction," *Current Psychiatry Reports,* Vol. 12, No. 5, October, 2010, pp. 462–470.

Iskender, Murat, and Ahmet Akin, "Social Self-Efficacy, Academic Locus of Control, and Internet Addiction," *Computers and Education*, Vol. 54, 2010, pp. 1101–1106.

Ivory, James D., and Sriram Kalyanaraman, "The Effects of Technological Advancement and Violent Content in Video Games on Players' Feelings of Presence, Involvement, Physiological Arousal, and Aggression," *Journal of Communication,* Vol. 57, No. 3, 2007, pp. 532–555.

Jackson, Linda A., Alexander Von Eye, Hiram E. Fitzgerald, Edward A. Witt, and Yong Zhao. "Internet Use, Videogame Playing and Cell Phone Use as Predictors of Children's Body Mass Index (BMI), Body Weight, Academic Performance, and Social and Overall Self-Esteem," *Computers in Human Behavior*, Vol. 27, No. 1, 2011, pp. 599–604.

Jäger, Susanne, Kai W. Müller, Christian Ruckes, Tobias Wittig, Anil Batra, Michael Musalek, Karl Mann, Klaus Wölfling, and Manfred E. Beutel, "Effects of a Manualized Short-Term Treatment of Internet and Computer Game Addiction (STICA): Study Protocol for a Randomized Controlled Trial," *Trials,* Vol. 13, 2012, p. 43.

Jia, Ronnie, and Heather H. Jia, "Factorial Validity of Problematic Internet Use Scales," *Computers in Human Behavior,* Vol. 25, No. 6, 2009, pp. 1335–1342.

Jiang, Jessie, "Inside China's Fight Against Internet Addiction," *TIME*, January 28, 2009.

Kakabadse, Nada K., Gayle Porter, and David Vance, "The Unbalanced High-Tech Life: Are Employers Liable?", *Strategic Change,* Vol. 18, No. 1–2, 2009, pp. 1–13. As of November 12, 2014:
http://dx.doi.org/10.1002/jsc.837

Kaneez, Fatima Shad, Kejing Zhu, Liming Tie, and Nurul Bahriah Haji Osman, "Is Cognitive Behavioral Therapy an Intervention for Possible Internet Addiction Disorder?", *Journal of Drug and Alcohol Research,* Vol. 2, 2013, pp. 1–9.

Kaskutas, Lee A., "Alcoholics Anonymous Effectiveness: Faith Meets Science," *Journal of Addictive Diseases,* Vol. 28, No. 2, 2009, pp. 145–157.

Khazaal, Yasser, Constantina Xirossavidou, Riaz Khan, Yves Edel, Fadi Zebouni, and Daniele Zullino, "Cognitive-Behavioral Treatments for 'Internet Addiction'" *The Open Addiction Journal,* Vol. 5, 2012, pp. 30–35.

Kim, Jong-Un, "The Effect of a R/T Group Counseling Program on the Internet Addiction Level and Self-Esteem of Internet Addiction University Students," *International Journal of Reality Therapy,* Vol. 27, 2008, pp. 4–12.

Kim, Kyunghee, Eunjung Ryu, Mi-Young Chon, Eun-Ja Yeun, So-Young Choi, Jeong-Seok Seo, and Bum-Woo Nam, "Internet Addiction in Korean Adolescents and its Relation to Depression and Suicidal Ideation: A Questionnaire Survey," *International Journal of Nursing Studies*, Vol. 43, No. 2, 2006, pp. 185–192.

Kim, Sun Mi, Doug Hyun Han, Young Sik Lee, and Perry F. Renshaw, "Combined Cognitive Behavioral Therapy and Bupropion for the Treatment of Problematic On-Line Game Play in Adolescents with Major Depressive Disorder," *Computers in Human Behavior,* Vol. 28, No. 5, September 2012, pp. 1954–1959. As of November 12, 2014: http://www.sciencedirect.com/science/article/pii/S0747563212001434

King, Daniel L., Paul H. Delfabbro, Mark D. Griffiths, and Michael Gradisar, "Assessing Clinical Trials of Internet Addiction Treatment: A Systematic Review and CONSORT Evaluation," *Clinical Psychology Review,* Vol. 31, No. 7, November 2011, pp. 1110–1116. As of November 12, 2014: http://www.sciencedirect.com/science/article/pii/S0272735811001085

Ko, Chih-Hung, Gin-Chung Liu, Sigmund Hsiao, Ju-Yu Yen, Ming-Jen Yang, Wei-Chen Lin, Cheng-Fang Yen, and Cheng-Sheng Chen, "Brain Activities Associated with Gaming Urge of Online Gaming Addiction," *Journal of Psychiatry Research*, Vol. 43, No. 7, 2009, pp. 739–747.

Ko, Chih-Hung, Ju-Yu Yen, Cheng-Sheng Chen, Yi-Chun Yeh, and Cheng-Fang Yen, "Predictive Values of Psychiatric Symptoms for Internet Addiction in Adolescents: A Two-Year Prospective Study," *Archives of Pediatric Adolescent Medicine,* Vol. 163, No. 10, 2009, pp. 937–943.

Ko, C.-H., J.-Y. Yen, C.-F. Yen, C.-S. Chen, C.-C. Chen, "The Association Between Internet Addiction and Psychiatric Disorder: A Review of the Literature," *European Psychiatry,* Vol. 27, 2012, pp. 1–8.

Ko, Chih-Hung, Ju-Yu Yen, Cheng-Fang Yen, Huang-Chi Lin, and Ming-Jen Yang, "Factors Predictive for Incidence and Remission of Internet Addiction in Young Adolescents: A Prospective Study," *CyberPsychology and Behavior,* Vol. 10, No. 4, 2007, pp. 545–551.

Kraut, Robert, Sara Kiesler, Bonka Boneva, Jonathon Cummings, Vicki Helgeson, and Anne Crawford, "Internet Paradox Revisited," *Journal of Social Issues,* Vol. 58, No. 1, 2002, pp. 49–74.

Kraut, Robert, Michael Patterson, Vicki Lundmark, Sara Kiesler, Tridas Mukophadhyay, and William Scherlis, "Internet Paradox: A Social Technology That Reduces Social Involvement and Psychological Well-Being?", *American Psychologist*, Vol. 53, No. 9, 1998, pp 1017–31.

Kubicek, Katrina, Julie Carpineto, Bryce McDavitt, George Weiss, and Michele D. Kipke, "Use and Perceptions of the Internet for Sexual Information and Partners: A Study of Young Men Who Have Sex with Men," *Archives Of Sexual Behavior,* Vol. 40, No. 4, 2011, pp. 803–816.

Kuss, D. J., M. D. Griffiths, L. Karila, and J. Billieux, "Internet Addiction: A Systematic Review of Epidemiological Research for the Last Decade," *Current Pharmaceutical Design*, August 29, 2013.

Kwon, Jung-Hye, "Toward the Prevention of Adolescent Internet Addiction," *Internet Addiction*, John Wiley and Sons, Inc., 2007, pp. 223–243. As of November 12, 2014: http://dx.doi.org/10.1002/9781118013991.ch13

Ladouceur, Robert, Caroline Sylvain, Claude Boutin, Stella Lachance, Celine Doucet, Jean Leblond, and Christian Jacques, "Cognitive Treatment of Pathological Gambling," *Journal of Nervous and Mental Disease,* Vol. 189, No. 11, November 2001, pp. 774–780.

Lal, Shalini, and Carol E. Adair, "E-Mental Health: A Rapid Review of the Literature," *Psychiatric Services,* Vol. 65, No. 1, January 1, 2014, pp. 24–32.

LaRose, Robert, Carolyn A. Lin, and Matthew S. Eastin, "Unregulated Internet Usage: Addiction, Habit, or Deficient Self-Regulation?", *Media Psychology,* Vol. 5, No. 3, August 1, 2003, pp. 225–253. As of November 12, 2014: http://dx.doi.org/10.1207/S1532785XMEP0503_01

Larose, Robert, Dana Mastro, and Matthew S. Eastin, "Understanding Internet Usage: A Social-Cognitive Approach to Uses and Gratifications," *Social Science Computer Review,* Vol. 19, No. 4, 2001, pp. 395–413. As of November 12, 2014: http://ssc.sagepub.com/content/19/4/395.abstract

Laudet, Alexandre B., "The Impact of Alcoholics Anonymous on Other Substance Abuse Related Twelve-Step Programs," in *Recent Developments in Alcoholism: Research on Alcoholics Anonymous and Spirituality in Addiction Recovery*, M. Galanter and L. A. Kaskutas, eds., New York: Springer, 2008, pp. 71–89.

Lee, Eun Jin, "A Case Study of Internet Game Addiction," *Journal of Addictions Nursing,* Vol. 22, No. 4, December 14, 2011, pp. 208–213. As of November 12, 2014: http://informahealthcare.com/doi/abs/10.3109/10884602.2011.616609

Li, Geng, and Xiu-Ying Dai, "Control Study of Cognitive-Behavior Therapy in Adolescents with Internet Addiction Disorder," *Chinese Mental Health Journal,* Vol. 23, No. 7, 2009, pp. 457–470.

Lin, I., C. H. Ko, Y. P. Chang, T. L. Liu, P. W. Wang, H. C. Lin, M. F. Huang, Y. C. Yeh, W. J. Chou, and C. F. Yen, "The Association Between Suicidality and Internet Addiction and Activities in Taiwanese Adolescents," *Comprehensive Psychiatry*, Vol. 55, No. 5, 2014, pp. 504–510.

Lin, Min-Pei, Huei-Chen Ko, and Jo Yung-Wei Wu, "Prevalence and Psychosocial Risk Factors Associated with Internet Addiction in a Nationally Representative Sample of College Students in Taiwan." *Cyberpsychology, Behavior, and Social Networking,* Vol. 14, No. 12, 2011, pp. 741–746.

Liu, Chennan, Minli Liao, and Douglas C. Smith, "An Empirical Review of Internet Addiction Outcome Studies in China," *Research on Social Work Practice,* Vol. 22, No. 3, 2012, pp. 282–292. As of November 12, 2014:
http://rsw.sagepub.com/content/22/3/282.abstract

Lortie, C. L., and M. J. Guitton. "Internet Addiction Assessment Tools: Dimensional Structure and Methodological Status," *Addiction,* Vol. 108, No. 7, 2013, pp. 1207–1216.

McHugh, R. Kathryn, Bridget A. Hearon, and Michael W. Otto, "Cognitive Behavioral Therapy for Substance Use Disorders," *Psychiatric Clinics of North America,* Vol. 33, No. 3, September 2010, pp. 511–525.

Messias, Erick, Juan Castro, Anil Saini, Manzoor Usman, and Dale Peeples, "Sadness, Suicide, and Their Association with Video Game and Internet Overuse Among Teens: Results from the Youth Risk Behavior Survey 2007 and 2009," *Suicide and Life-Threatening Behavior*, Vol. 41, No. 3, 2011, pp. 307–315.

Miller, Laura L., Laurie T. Martin, Douglas Yeung, Matthew D. Trujillo, and Martha J. Timmer, *Information and Communication Technologies to Promote Social and Psychological Well-Being in the Air Force: A 2012 Survey of Airmen*, Santa Monica, Calif.: RAND Corporation, RR-695-AF, 2014. As of December 12, 2014:
http://www.rand.org/pubs/research_reports/RR695.html

Moreno, Megan A., Lauren Jelenchick, Elizabeth Cox, Henry Young, and Dimitri A. Christakis, "Problematic Internet Use Among U.S. Youth: A Systematic Review," *Archives of Pediatrics and Adolescent Medicine,* 2011, Vol. 165, No. 9, pp. 797–805.

Mythily, Subramaniam, Shijia Qiu, and Munidasa Winslow, "Prevalence and Correlates of Excessive Internet Use Among Youth in Singapore," *Annals of the Academy of Medicine Singapore*, Vol. 37, No. 1, 2008, pp. 9–14.

Olatunji, Bunmi O., Josh M. Cisler, and Brett J. Deacon, "Efficacy of Cognitive Behavioral Therapy for Anxiety Disorders: A Review of Meta-Analytic Findings," *Psychiatric Clinics of North America,* Vol. 33, No. 3, September 2010, pp. 557–577.

Orzack, M. H., and D. S. Orzack, "Treatment of Computer Addicts with Complex Co-Morbid Psychiatric Disorders," *Cyberpsychology and Behavior,* Vol. 2, No. 5, 1999, pp. 465–473.

Orzack, Maressa Hecht, Andrew C. Voluse, David Wolf, and John Hennen, "An Ongoing Study of Group Treatment for Men Involved in Problematic Internet-Enabled Sexual Behavior," *Cyberpsychology and Behavior,* Vol. 9, No. 3, June 2006, pp. 348–360.

Pallesen, Ståle, Morten Mitsem, Gerd Kvale, Bjørn-Helge Johnsen, and Helge Molde, "Outcome of Psychological Treatments of Pathological Gambling: A Review and Meta-Analysis," *Addiction,* Vol. 100, No. 10, 2005, pp. 1412–1422. As of November 12, 2014: http://dx.doi.org/10.1111/j.1360-0443.2005.01204.x

Pampallona, Sandro, Paola Bollini, Giuseppe Tibaldi, Bruce Kupelnick, and Carmine Munizza, "Combined Pharmacotherapy and Psychological Treatment for Depression: A Systematic Review," *Archives of General Psychiatry,* Vol. 61, No. 7, July 2004, pp. 714–719.

Pemberton, Michael R., Jason Williams, Mindy Herman-Stahl, Sara L. Calvin, Michael R. Bradshaw, Robert M. Bray, Jamie L. Ridenhour, Royer Cook, Rebekah K. Hersch, Reid K. Hester, and Glenda M. Mitchell, "Evaluation of Two Web-Based Alcohol Interventions in the U.S. Military," *Journal of Studies on Alcohol and Drugs,* Vol. 72, No. 3, 2011, pp. 480–489.

Petersen, K. U., N. Weymann, Y. Schelb, R. Thiel, and R. Thomasius, "Pathological Internet Use—Epidemiology, Diagnostics, Co-Occurring Disorders and Treatment," *Fortschritte der Neurologie-Psychiatrie,* Vol. 77, No. 5, May 2009, pp. 263–271. As of November 12, 2014: http://europepmc.org/abstract/MED/19418384

Petry, Nancy M., "Gamblers Anonymous and Cognitive-Behavioral Therapies for Pathological Gamblers," *Journal of Gambling Studies,* Vol. 21, No. 1, March 1, 2005, pp. 27–33. As of November 12, 2014: http://dx.doi.org/10.1007/s10899-004-1919-5

Petry, Nancy M., Florian Rehbein, Douglas A. Gentile, Jeroen S. Lemmens, Hans-Jürgen Rumpf, Thomas Mößle, Gallus Bischof, Ran Tao, Daniel S. S. Fung, Guilherme Borges, Marc Auriacombe, Angels Gonzálex Ibáñez, Philip Tam, and Charles P. O'Brien, "An International Consensus for Assessing Internet Gaming Disorder Using the New DSM-5 Approach," *Addiction,* January 23, 2014.

Pew Research Center, "Three Technology Revolutions," 2014a. As of November 12, 2014: http://www.pewInternet.org/three-technology-revolutions/

Pew Research Center, *The Web at 25 in the U.S.,* 2014b. As of November 12, 2014: http://www.pewInternet.org/2014/02/25/the-web-at-25-in-the-u-s

Pietrzak, Robert, Douglas Johnson, Marc Goldstein, James Malley, and Steven Southwick, "Perceived Stigma And Barriers To Mental Health Care Utilization Among OEF-OIF Veterans," *Psychiatric Services,* Vol. 60, No. 8, August 2009, pp. 1118–1122. As of November 13, 2014:
http://www.ncbi.nlm.nih.gov/pubmed/19648201

Prochaska, James O., and Charles C. DiClemente, "The transtheoretical approach," in *Handbook Of Psychotherapy Integration*, J. C. Norcross and M.R. Goldfried, eds., New York: Oxford University Press, 2005, pp. 147–171.

Pull, Charles B., "Self-Help Internet Interventions for Mental Disorders," *Current Opinion in Psychiatry,* Vol. 19, No. 1, January 2006, pp. 50–53.

Rooij, Antonius J., Mieke F. Zinn, Tim M. Schoenmakers, and Dike Mheen, "Treating Internet Addiction with Cognitive-Behavioral Therapy: A Thematic Analysis of the Experiences of Therapists," *International Journal of Mental Health and Addiction,* Vol. 10, No. 1, February 1, 2012, pp. 69–82. As of November 13, 2014:
http://dx.doi.org/10.1007/s11469-010-9295-0

Saisan, Joanna, Melinda Smith, Lawrence Robinson, and Jeanne Segal, "Internet and Computer Addiction Signs, Symptoms, and Treatment," HelpGuide.org, web page, undated. As of November 13, 2014:
http://www.helpguide.org/articles/addiction/internet-and-computer-addiction.htm

Saleem, Muniba, Craig A. Anderson, and Douglas A. Gentile, "Effects Of Prosocial, Neutral, and Violent Video Games on College Students' Affect," *Aggressive Behavior,* Vol. 38, No. 4, May 2012, pp. 263–271.

Schell, T. L., and G. N. Marshall, "Survey of Individuals Previously Deployed for OEF/OIF," in *Invisible Wounds of War: Psychological and Cognitive Injuries, Their Consequences, and Services to Assist Recovery*, T. Tanielian and L. H. Jaycox, eds., Santa Monica, Calif.: RAND Corporation, MG-720-CCF, 2008. As of November 13, 2014:
http://www.rand.org/pubs/monographs/MG720.html

Scherer, Kathy, "College Life Online: Healthy and Unhealthy Internet Use," *Journal of College Development*, Vol. 38, 1997, pp. 655–665.

Shapira, Nathan A., Mary C. Lessig, Toby D. Goldsmith, Steven T. Szabo, Martin Lazoritz, Mark S. Gold, and Dan J. Stein, "Problematic Internet Use: Proposed Classification and Diagnostic Criteria," *Depression and Anxiety*, Vol. 17, No. 4, 2003, pp. 207–216.

Shaw, M., and D. W. Black, "Internet Addiction: Definition, Assessment, Epidemiology and Clinical Management," *CNS Drugs*, Vol. 22, No. 5, 2008, pp. 353–365.

Shek, D. T., V. M. Tang, and C. Y. Lo, "Evaluation of an Internet Addiction Treatment Program for Chinese Adolescents in Hong Kong" *Adolescence*, Vol. 44, No. 174, Summer 2009, pp. 359–373.

Shotton, Margaret A., *Computer Addiction? A Study of Computer Dependency*. London, United Kingdom: Taylor and Francis, 1989.

Shotton, Margaret A., "The Costs and Benefits Of 'Computer Addiction'," *Behaviour and Information Technology*, Vol. 10, No. 3, 1991, pp. 219–230.

Siomos, K., V. Dafoulis, G. Floros, I. Karagiannaki-Kastani, and K. Christianopoulos, "Presentation of a Specialized Outpatient Unit for Internet and PC Addiction—First Year of Operations, Results, Recommendations for the Future, *European Psychiatry*, Vol. 25, Supplement 1, 2010.

Siomos, K., G. Floros, D. Braimiotis, A. Lappas, and I. Karagiannaki-Kastani, I., "Stress-Related, Self-Inflicted Wounds Furing On-Line Gaming: Diagnosis, Co-Morbidity and Treatment, *European Psychiatry*, Vol. 25, Supplement 1, 2010.

Stanton, J. M., and E. M. Weiss, "Electronic Monitoring in Their Own Words: An Exploratory Study of Employees' Experiences with New Types of Surveillance," *Computers in Human Behavior*, Vol. 16, No. 4, July 2000, pp. 423–440.

Su, W., X. Fang, J. K. Miller, and Y. Wang, "Internet-Based Intervention for the Treatment of Online Addiction for College Students in China: A Pilot Study of the Healthy Online Self-Helping Center," *Cyberpsychology, Behavior, and Social Networking*, Vol. 14, No. 9, 2011, pp. 497–503.

Suler, John R., "To Get What You Need: Healthy and Pathological Internet Use," *Cyberpsychology and Behavior*, Vol. 2, No. 5, 1999. pp. 355–393.

Sylvain, C., R. Ladouceur, and J. M. Boisvert, "Cognitive and Behavioral Treatment of Pathological Gambling: A Controlled Study. *Journal of Consulting and Clinical Psychology*, Vol. 65, No. 5 1997, pp. 727–732.

Tait, R. J., and H. Christensen, "Internet-Based Interventions for Young People with Problematic Substance Use: A Systematic Review," *Medical Journal of Australia*, Vol. 192, No. 11 Suppl., S15-21, 2010.

Thatcher, Andrew, and Shamira Goolam, "Development And Psychometric Properties Of The Problematic Internet Use Questionnaire," *South African Journal of Psychology*, Vol. 35, 2005, pp. 793–809.

Twohig, M. P., and J. M. Crosby, "Acceptance and Commitment Therapy as a Treatment for Problematic Internet Pornography Viewing," *Behavior Therapy*, Vol. 41, No. 3, 2010, pp. 285–295.

Urbaczewski, Andrew, and Leonard M. Jessup, "Does Electronic Monitoring of Employee Internet Usage Work? *Commununications of the Association for Computing Machinery,* Vol 45, No. 1, 2002, pp. 80–83.

Vitiello, B., "Combined Cognitive-Behavioural Therapy and Pharmacotherapy for Adolescent Depression: Does It Improve Outcomes Compared with Monotherapy?" *CNS Drugs,* Vol. 23, No. 4, 2009, pp. 271–280.

Vogt, D., "Mental Health-Related Beliefs as a Barrier to Service Use for Military Personnel and Veterans: A Review," *Psychiatric Services,* Vol. 62, No. 2, 2011, pp. 135–142.

Weinstein, Aviv, and Mitchel Lejoyeux, "Internet Addiction or Excessive Internet Use," *The American Journal of Drug and Alcohol Abuse,* Vol. 36, 2010, pp. 277–283.

Williams, Dmitri, Nick Yee, and Scott E. Caplan, "Who Plays, How Much, And Why? Debunking The Stereotypical Gamer Profile," *Journal of Computer-Mediated Communication,* Vol. 13, No. 4, 2008, pp. 993–1018.

Williams, J., M. Herman-Stahl, S. L. Calvin, M. Pemberton, and M. Bradshaw, "Mediating Mechanisms of a Military Web-Based Alcohol Intervention," *Drug and Alcohol Dependence,* Vol. 100, No. 3, 2009, pp. 248–257.

Winkler, Alexander, Beate Dörsing, Winfied Rief, Yuhui Shen, and Julia A. Glombiewski, "Treatment of Internet Addiction: A Meta-Analysis, *Clinical Psychology Review,* Vol. 33, No. 2, 2013, pp. 317–329.

Wölfling, K. J., K. W. Müller, and M. E. Beutel, "Treating Internet Addiction: First Results on Efficacy of a Standardized Cognitive-Behavioral Therapeutic Approach, *European Psychiatry,* Vol. 27, Supplement 1, 2012.

Wood, Robert T., and Robert J. Williams, "A Comparative Profile Of The Internet Gambler: Demographic Characteristics, Game-Play Patterns, and Problematic Gambling Status," *New Media Society,* Vol. 13, No. 7, 2011, pp. 1123–1141.

Yang, Chang-Kook. "Sociopsychiatric Characteristics of Adolescents Who Use Computers to Excess," *Acta Psychiatrica Scandinavica,* Vol. 104, No. 3, 2001, pp. 217–222.

Yates, Tuppett M., Margo A. Gregor, and Mark G. Haviland, "Child Maltreatment, Alexithymia, and Problematic Internet Use in Young Adulthood," *Cyberpsychology, Behavior, and Social Networking,* Vol. 15, No. 4, 2012, pp. 219–225.

Ybarra, M. L., and W. W. Eaton, "Internet-Based Mental Health Interventions, *Mental Health Services Research,* Vol. 7, No. 2, 2005, pp. 75–87.

Yen, Ju-Yu, Chih-Hung Ko, Cheng-Fang Yen, Hsiu-Yueh Wu, and Ming-Jen Yang, "The Comorbid Psychiatric Symptoms of Internet Addiction: Attention Deficit and Hyperactivity

Disorder (ADHD), Depression, social Phobia, and Hostility," *Journal of Adolescent Health*, Vol. 41, 2007, pp. 93–98.

Young, Kimberly S., "Internet Addiction: The Emergence of a New Clinical Disorder," *Cyberpsychology and Behavior,* Vol. 1, No. 3, 1998, pp. 237–244.

Young, K. S., "Internet Addiction: Symptoms, Evaluation, and Treatment," in *Innovations in Clinical Practice* (Volume 17), L. VandeCreek and T. L. Jackson, eds., Sarasota, Fla.: Professional Resource Press, 1999.

Young, Kimberly S., "Internet Addiction: A New Clinical Phenomenon and Its Consequences," *American Behavioral Scientist*, Vol. 48, No. 4, 2004, pp. 402–415.

Young, K. S., "Cognitive Behavior Therapy with Internet Addicts: Treatment Outcomes and Implications, *Cyberpsychology and Behavior,* Vol. 10, No. 5, 2007, pp. 671–679.

Young, Kimberly, "Policies and Procedures to Manage Employee Internet Abuse," *Computers in Human Behavior,* Vol., 26, No. 6, 2010, pp. 1467–1471.

Young, K. S., "Treatment Outcomes Using CBT-IA with Internet-Addicted Patients, *Journal of Behavioral Addictions,* Vol. 2, 2013, pp 209–215.

Young, Kimberly S., and Carl J. Case, "Internet Abuse in the Workplace: New Trends in Risk Management," *CyberPsychology and Behavior,* Vol. 7, No. 1, 2004, pp. 105–111.

Young, K. S., and C. N. de Abreu, *Internet Addiction: A Handbook and Guide to Evaluation and Treatment*. Hoboken, N.J.: John Wiley and Sons, Inc., 2011.

Young, Kimberly S., Xiao D. Yue, and Li Ying. "Prevalence Estimates And Etiological Models Of Internet Addiction." In *Internet Addiction: A Handbook And Guide To Evaluation And Treatment*, K. S. Young and C. N. de Abreu, eds., Hoboken, N.J.: John Wiley and Sons, Inc, 2011.

Zhu, T. M., R. J. Jin, X. M. Zhong, J. Chen, and H. Li, ["Effects of Electroacupuncture Combined with Psychologic Interference on Anxiety State and Serum NE Content in the Patient of Internet Addiction Disorder"], *Zhongguo Zhen Jiu*, Vol. 28, No. 8, 2008, pp. 561–564.

Zhu, T. M., H. Li, Y.P. Du, Z. Zheng, and R. J. Jin, ["Intervention on Network Craving and Encephalofluctuogram in Patients with Internet Addiction Disorder: A Randomized Controlled Trial"], *Zhongguo Zhen Jiu,* Vol. 31, No. 5, 2011, pp. 395–399.

Zhu, T. M., H. Li, R. J. Jin, Z. Zheng, Y. Luo, H. Ye, and H. M. Zhu, "Effects of Electroacupuncture Combined Psycho-Intervention on Cognitive Function and Event-Related Potentials P300 and Mismatch Negativity in Patients with Internet Addiction," *Chinese Journal of Integrated Medicine, Vol. 18, No. 2,* 2012, pp. 146–151.

Zur Institute, *Certificate Program in Psychology of the Web*, online continuing education course, 2014. As of November 11, 2014:
http://www.zurinstitute.com/certificateininternetaddiction.html